# So You Think You Want to Restore an Old Ford..

## A Memoir

This is a nostalgic memoir of growing up in the late 1940s to the mid-1950s, and the impact of automobile designs on the author. His latent passion for old cars was awakened later in life, and he proceeded to restore an old Ford.

GR Dornfeld

Introduction

GR Dornfeld earned a BS degree in Aeronautical Engineering from Boston University as well as a commission as a 2/Lt. in the Air Force Reserve in June 1960. He performed as a crew navigator in Strategic Air Command KC-97G air refueling tankers for five years, before leaving active duty to work as an aerospace engineer in private industry, first for Hamilton Standard in aircraft propellers for four years and then for GE jet engines for the next 31 years. In industry, he honed skills designing hardware for jet engines while developing sensitivity about aircraft engine maintainability issues. This was where he started working on cars as a "backyard mechanic." As indicated within, his latent interest in antique cars was awakened while attending an offsite seminar in Interpersonal Awareness.

Preface

This book is a memoir dedicated to my fascination with cars of the late 1940s and through the mid-1950s. I was born in 1939, so by the time I was aware of cars, I was already six years old, and the post-war models were just coming out. I wrote this book to bring back memories of the car designs and driving experiences of that era.

My family could not afford a car while I was growing up. In high school, the car of my dreams was a 1950 Ford convertible. This was in 1953 through 1956. The car would have a high-gloss black lacquer paint job, rear wheel skirts with paint to match the body and wide whitewall tires (WWW tires). There would be dual exhaust with Smithie mufflers and chrome exhaust tips. In order to make the car look cool, it would be lowered in the rear. Under the hood, the Ford flathead V-8 engine would have finned aluminum heads to aid in engine cooling (and make the engine better looking, also). There would be lots of chromed engine accessories, such as the generator housing, water pump, and radiator hoses (chrome steel pipes over the rubber radiator hoses). There would be twin carburetors with a chrome intake manifold set up to mount the twin carburetors.

I actually purchased the first car in my immediate family, a well-worn and used 1949 Pontiac fastback, with the straight-eight engine and standard three-speed transmission. I sold it about a year later to purchase a used 1950 Mercury coupe, with the sweet sounding flathead V-8 engine.

Much later in life, I discovered a latent passion for old cars. In 1979, I bought a rotted-out 1939 Ford Convertible Coupe Deluxe and, over seven years, restored the car with the help of my son, Scott, and a talented restoration shop.

The restoration process isn't for everyone, but the book can be enjoyed by all who even thought about restoring an old car.

Table of Contents

# Chapter 1    Cars of My Youth, 1949 through 1956

<u>Reminiscing about cars of that era</u>
I was born in 1939, and was crazy about cars as I grew up. My family was poor, and did not own a car. There was no father figure in my household, so there was nobody to show me how to use tools to work on a car. My tool inventory consisted of one wooden handled blade screwdriver and a small ball peen hammer. However, I read everything in the library about the mechanics of an automobile. Two magazines of the day, Mechanics Illustrated and Popular Science, provided me with information about car mechanics. I remember reading a Popular Mechanics issue in 1953. The article described the new 1954 Ford Y-block overhead valve V-8 and the new ball-joint front end suspension. When the new-model cars were introduced each year, I visited the dealerships to see them for myself.

The late 1940s to the early 1950s were a transition period for American auto designs. I could not see it at the time, because I did not have the benefit of hindsight.

<u>The Times</u>
World War II ended. Those families lucky enough to have owned a car before the war either put the car in storage for the duration, or drove it into the ground using rationed gasoline and well-worn tires. By 1945, Americans returning from the war and those from the home front were hungry for new cars. The auto manufacturers rushed to produce warmed-over pre-war models, just to get cars into the pipeline, until new designs could be introduced.

The following is intended to hit the highlights of the car designs that were produced from immediately post-war to 1956. After 1956, with the exception of the 1957 Chevrolet, I lost interest in the designs. In the interest of brevity, I cover only Chrysler, Ford and Chevrolet. The intent is to demonstrate the rapid design changes in this time period. The old six-cylinder and straight-eight engines were replaced with the overhead valve design V-8, standard transmissions were replaced with automatic transmissions, and power accessories and air conditioning were introduced.

Chrysler:[i]

Post-war; 1946-1948; unlike most car companies, Chrysler did not make major changes with each model year from 1946 through 1948. As a result, models for 1946 through 1948 had the same basic appearance, with their "harmonica" grille, based on the body introduced with the 1941 models. 1947 saw a minor redesign in tires, trim, and instrument panel, while the first 1948s were just 1947s with no visible changes.

Post-war Chryslers continued to offer Fluid Drive, which was a semi-automatic transmission.

1949-1950 Chrysler; the 1949 – 1950 Chrysler was available with the 325.5 cubic inch displacement (cid) straight-eight engine. A six-cylinder engine was also available. The transmission was Fluid Drive with Prestomatic semi-automatic transmission. The 1950 Chrysler introduced their two-door hardtop (the same year that GM manufacturers brought out their hardtop models) and foam padding on the dash for safety.

In 1951, Chrysler introduced its 180 horsepower (HP) FirePower Hemi (hemispherical combustion chambers) V-8 engine. This was a powerhouse for its day, logging an acceleration of 0-60 miles per hour (mph) time of 10 seconds. This was faster than the Oldsmobile Rocket 88 303 cid-powered car. Power steering was offered in Chryslers with the Hemi engine. It was called "Hydraglide."

1953; this year was notable for the one-piece curved windshield and rear fenders integrated into the body.

1954; the 1954 was a premium version of a standard 1950s size body. Chrysler's interest in six-cylinder vehicles began to wane in favor of the popular FirePower Hemi V-8. The standard model had a mild 195 HP output while the DeLuxe was used as a test-bed of the engine's capabilities by outputting 235 HP. (Such power was unheard of in 1954 from its competitors.)

Although introduced very late in the 1953 model year, all 1954 New Yorkers were available with the new two-speed Powerflite automatic transmission. Fluid-Torque-Drive and Fluid-Matic were dropped.

1955;          the hemi engine produced 250 HP this year. The result would become an ongoing trend for increasing engine output throughout the next two decades with Chrysler and its rival competitors. The Powerflite transmission was controlled by a lever on the instrument panel.

Post-War designs were warmed over Pre-War

Pre-War 1941 Chrysler                                    1948 Chrysler

1951 Chrysler                                    1955 Chrysler

Chrysler Photos[1]

1956;          Chrysler christened this model year "PowerStyle." The New Yorker gained a new mesh grille, leather seats, pushbutton PowerFlite selector, and a V8 with 280 HP. This was the first year for the New Yorker 4-door pillarless hardtop.

# Ford[2]

1946;          the 1946 Ford was identical to the 1942 model under the skin, though a heavy new grille with horizontal bars and red accents modernized the car somewhat. One notable change was to use the 239 cid engine which since 1939 had been used in Mercurys and trucks. The engine was capable of 100 HP for the first time.

---

1

2

1947;          for the first few weeks, the 1947 model was identical to the 1946. Ford then restyled the body slightly, first by moving the parking lights from above the grill to below each headlight. Exterior moldings were changed from grooved to a smooth design. A new hood ornament with a blue plastic insert was installed. New hubcap design became available in March. Interior dash color was changed from red accent to gold. By September the roof mounted antenna was moved to the cowl. Horns were moved to in front of the radiator from the engine compartment. The final 1947 models were titled in November.

1948;          this was the final year for the old-style Ford, with an all-new model launched partway through the year.

1949;          the 1949 Ford was the first all-new automobile design introduced by the Big Three (Chrysler Corporation, General Motors Corporation and Ford Motor Company) after World War II. Popularly called the "Shoebox Ford" for its slab-sided design, the 1949 Ford was credited both with saving Ford and ushering in modern streamlined car design with changes such as integrated fenders. The design would continue through the 1951 model year.

Save for its drivetrain, this was an all-new car in every way, with a modern ladder-frame now supporting a coil spring suspension in front and longitudinal semi-elliptical springs in back. The engine was moved forward to make more room in the passenger compartment and the antiquated torque tube was replaced by a modern open drive shaft. Ford's popular 226 cid straight-6 and 239 cid Flathead V8 remained, now rated at 90 HP and 100 HP, respectively.

1950;          this year saw a new Crestliner "Sports Sedan" — a 2-door sedan with 2-tone paint, intended to battle Chevrolet's popular hardtop coupe of 1950. The 1949 and 1950 styling was similar, with a single central "bullet" in the frowning chrome grille. In the center there was a red space that had either a 6 or 8 depending if the car had the six-cylinder engine or the V8.

1951;         Fords featured an optional Ford-O-Matic three speed automatic transmission for the first time. Ford finally answered the Chevrolet Bel Air charge with the Victoria hardtop in 1951. The car was an instant hit, outselling the Chevy by nearly 10%. The Crestliner continued for one more year, however. All 1951 Fords sported a new "dual-bullet" grille and heavy chrome bumpers. This year Ford also added a new "turn-key" ignition. Front suspension was independent coil springs.

1952;         The Ford line of cars was again refreshed for 1952, although remaining similar to the all-new 1949 Fords. This time, curved one-piece windshield glass joined a new "Mileage Maker" straight-6 engine with 101 HP.

Post-War models were Warmed over Pre-War models

Pre-War 1942 Ford

Post-War 1946 Ford Coupe

First Post-War Redesign
1950 Ford

1952 Ford Coupe

1955 Ford Crown Victoria

Ford Grouping[3]

3

1953;        1953 was Ford's 50th anniversary. The big news for 1953 was the availability of power-assisted brakes and steering, which had previously been limited to the Mercury and Lincoln lines. The center grill bullet lost its ring and was now flanked by vertical black stripes, while the corner markers were plain rectangular lights rather than the circular "intakes." All 1953 Fords featured commemorative steering wheels marking the company's 50th anniversary. Toward the end of the year, Ford added "Master-Guide" power steering as an option on cars with V8s.

1954;        The long-lived Flathead V8 engine was replaced for 1954 by a 239 cid overhead valve Y-block unit, marking the end of an era. This engine produced 130 HP with a 2-barrel carburetor. The six-cylinder was up to 223 cid and now produced 115 hp. Another new addition was the "Crestline Skyliner" 2-door hardtop, which featured an acrylic glass panel over the front half of the roof. Also added was the new "Astra-Dial Control Panel" Speedometer, which had a clear, plastic covering on the top, which let sunlight illuminate it in the day-time.

1955 Ford[4]

The following is an extensive write-up on the 1955 Ford because Ford produced an exciting design, in my opinion.

There was a new body for 1955 to keep up with surging Chevrolet, although it remained similar to the 1952 Ford underneath. The Mileage Maker I6 was bumped up to 223 cid for 120 HP and the new-for-1954 Y-block V8 was now offered in two sizes: Standard Fords used a 272 cid version with 162 HP with 2-barrel carburetor and single exhaust or 182 HP with 4-barrel carburetor and dual exhaust, but the large 292 CID unit from the Thunderbird was also offered, boasting 193 HP

There was a new Crown Victoria-style featuring a chrome "basket handle" across the familiar (and continued) "Victoria" hardtop roof. The "Skyliner" acrylic glass roof was still offered, this time only on the Crown Victoria model.

---

There was also the panoramic windshield found on Oldsmobiles, Buicks and Cadillacs the previous year. With this panoramic windshield the A-pillars had a vertical angle. This gave the driver more panoramic visibility.

For the first time, seat belts were offered as a dealer option (not factory installed, with instructions provided by a Service Bulletin). Also new for 1955 was Ford's first factory installed air conditioner.

1956;          the egg crate grille featured on the 1955 cars was widened into a series of rectangles for 1956. Also, there was the adoption of a 12-volt electrical system across the line. The Crown Victoria Skyliner's sales plummeted with just 603 made, and it was replaced by a convertible the next year. A new addition at midyear was the "Town Victoria" 4-door hardtop model which, along with the new Customline Victoria 2-door hardtop, were meant to compete with the Chevrolet Bel Air. Idiot lights for oil pressure and ammeter were standard.

Victoria hardtop coupes now adopted the lower, sleeker roofline used by both 1955 and 1956 Crown Victoria, sans the wide chrome roof trim.

The Lifeguard safety package, consisting of seat belts, padded dashboard, deep-dish steering wheel, and a breakaway rear-view mirror, was introduced. The option was a slow-seller. The optional air conditioner, which remained expensive and thus a slow seller, was totally revamped; the compressor was now housed beneath the hood and the cooling vents were moved to atop the dashboard (it could not be ordered on the Thunderbird).

## Chevrolet[5]

The 1946, 1947 and 1948 Chevrolet automobiles were relatively unchanged from one another, and were essentially warmed over pre-war models.

In the 1941/42 model years, the 216 cid inline 6 "Blue Flame" engine was the only one offered. It produced 85 horsepower at 3300 rpm. In 1947 output was bumped up to 90 horsepower. A Deluxe of

5

this vintage could easily exceed 80 miles per hour without overdrive. The transmission was a manual synchromesh 3 speed, with vacuum assisted shift, in which the "three-on-the-tree" shifter was able to be moved between gears by the slightest pressure on the lever. Overdrive was a rare option. Connection to the third member rear-end was via an enclosed "torque tube" driveshaft. In 1949, all the Chevrolets got the first new styling after the war. The Deluxe was the brand new upper-end model for Chevy. The cheapest Deluxe was the Deluxe Styleline 6-passenger sedan, costing $1,492.

In 1950, not much had changed. For 1951, there were few styling changes to the outside, though the dash was completely new.

For 1950, Chevrolet came up with a revolutionary style that would set a pattern for decades. The Bel Air Hardtop was styled as a convertible with a *non-detachable* solid roof. Models like this had been around since the 1920s, including early Chevrolets, with no degree of success. But the newly revised idea, sweeping the GM line from Chevrolet to Cadillac, had finally found its era. First year production reached only 76,662 as buyers cautiously tested the revised concept. The car cost $1,741 and weighed 3,225 pounds Front suspension was independent, and named "knee-action"

1941 Chevrolet

Post-War models were Warmed over Pre-war

1947 Chevrolet

First Major Body Style Change Post-War 1949 Chevrolet

1954 Chevrolet

1956 Chevrolet

Chevrolet Grouping[6]
The 1949 Chevrolet photo is by the author

The first Bel Airs of this era shared only their front sheet metal ahead of the A pillar with the rest of the range. The windshield, doors, glass, and trunk were common with the Styleline Deluxe Convertible Coupe; however the roof, rear quarters and rear windows were unique. The chassis and mechanicals were common with the rest of the passenger car range, and the overall appearance was the same except that the roof line was lower and the unique three piece rear screen gave it a longer and more balanced look. The first Bel Airs were available only with the premium trim level and specification, and therefore were not designated as either Special or Deluxe by Chevrolet. They did however have all the trim features and details common to the Deluxe models of the range.

Apart from the usual annual grille and trim changes, the 1951-52 Bel Air differs from the earlier 50 model with introduction of the higher and squarer rear guards that were across the whole range. The 1951 model introduced the Powerglide two-speed automatic transmission.

In 1953, Chevrolet renamed its series and the Bel Air name was applied to the premium model range. Two lower series, the 150 and 210, also emerged (as successors to the Special and Deluxe series, respectively). The 1953 Chevrolet was advertised as "Entirely new through and through," due to the restyled body panels, front and rear ends. However, essentially these Chevrolets had similar frame and mechanicals to the 1949-52 cars. The pre-war technology, such as torque-tube drive, six-cylinder splash-feed engines, knee action suspension, split windshields, etc., of the early models was phased out and the foundations for the first post war modern Chevrolet passenger car were finalized in this 53-54 model.

Of all the Bel Air variants available across the 53-54 range, the two door hardtop and convertible remain the stand outs in terms of style. 1953 was the first year for a curved, one-piece windshield.

1954;        For 1954, the Bel Air stayed essentially the same, except for a revised grille and taillights, and a revised engine that had insert bearings and higher oil pressure, needed for the full-flow oil filtration system that was not available prior to 1954. Prior to 1954, the 235 and 216 cid six-cylinder engines had babbit bearings and scoops to create oil pressure at the bottom of each rod and the oil pressure was standard at 15-30 PSI. During these years, there were three engine choices, depending on the transmission ordered. Both 235 cubic inch engines were "Blue Flame" inline six-cylinder OHV engines, featuring hydraulic valve lifters (in 1953 with automatic transmissions) and aluminum pistons. The 106 HP 235 cid engine was standard on stick shift models, with solid lifters and splash plus pressure lubrication including babbit bearings. Powerglide (two-speed automatic transmission) cars got a 115 HP version which had hydraulic lifters and full pressure lubrication.

1955;           The Chevrolet's full-size model received all new styling and power. It was called the "Hot One" in GM's advertising campaign. Chevrolet's styling was crisp, clean and incorporated a Ferrari-inspired grille. Bel Airs came with features found on cars in the lower model ranges plus interior carpet, chrome headliner bands on hardtops, chrome spears on front fenders, stainless steel window moldings and full wheel covers.

 Chevrolets gained a V8 engine option. and the option of the 2-speed automatic transmission, Powerglide, or a three speed manual transmission with optional overdrive. The new 265 cid V8 featured a modern, overhead valve high compression, short-stroke design that was so good that it remained in production in various displacements for many decades. The base V8 had a two-barrel carburetor and was rated at 162 HP. The "Power Pack" option featured a four-barrel carburetor and other upgrades yielding 180 HP. Later in the year, a "Super Power Pack" option added high-compression and a further 15 HP. "Idiot" lights replaced gauges for the generator and oil pressure.

Motor Trend magazine gave the Bel Air top marks for handling. Popular Mechanics reported acceleration for a V8 Bel Air with Powerglide as being 0-60 mph in 12.9 seconds, plus a comfortable ride, and good visibility. On the other hand, the horn ring blocked some of the speedometer, regular gasoline made the engine knock, and the first V8 engine off the line burned too much oil. A new option for V8-equipped 1955 models was air conditioning, with outlets on each side of the dashboard; a heavy-duty generator was included on cars equipped with this option.

1956;           Bel Air received a face-lift with a more conventional full-width grille, pleasing those customers who didn't favor the

Ferrari-inspired '55 front end. Distinctive two-tone body-side treatments and graceful front and rear wheel openings completed the "speedline" restyling. Single housings incorporated the taillight, stoplight, and backup light, and the left one held the gas filler - an idea popularized on Cadillacs. Among the seven Bel Air models was a new Sport Sedan, a pillarless four-door hardtop that looked handsome with all the windows rolled down and allowed easy entry into the back seat. Production exceeded 103,000, compared to 128,000 two-door hardtops. Shapely two-door Nomad wagons topped the price chart at $2,608, but now carried the same interior and rear-wheel sheet metal as other Bel Airs, lacking the original's unique trim. Seatbelts, shoulder harnesses, and a padded dashboard were available, and full-size cars could even get the hot Corvette 225-horsepower engine.

1957;          Engine displacement grew to 283 cid with the "Super Turbo Fire V8" option producing 283 HP with the help of continuous (closed loop) mechanical fuel injection. These so-called "fuelie" cars are quite rare, since most Bel Airs were fitted with carburetion. The 1957 Bel Air is among the most recognizable American cars of all time; well-maintained examples, especially Sport Coupes and Convertibles are highly sought after by collectors and enthusiasts. They are roomy, with tastefully restrained, period use tail fins and chrome. A second automatic transmission, Turboglide, was optional. While the original two-speed Powerglide continued unchanged, Turboglide provided a continuously variable gear ratio which made "shifting" imperceptible.

The New-Car Field Consolidated
In my lifetime, I have witnessed 15 major automobile makes expire: Saturn, Oldsmobile, Pontiac, Hummer, Studebaker, Packard, Kaiser, Fraser, Plymouth, De Soto, Edsel, Crosley, Henry J, Tucker and Mercury.

There were several other marques that became extinct, but they played a small part in the progress of automobile design. They were Amphicar, King Midget, Playboy and Aerocar, among others.

Amphicar

King Midget

Amphicar and King Midget[7]

## My memories of exciting innovations in new cars of the 1950s
The alternator came into its own. The advantage of the alternator was it charged the battery when the engine was at idle speed, whereas the generator did not. By the mid-1950s, the six volt electrical system was history. Twelve volt systems became standard.

Four barrel carburetors started replacing the two barrel models for extra high-end power. Automatic chokes became standard on carburetors.

The king pin front suspension became obsolete. In its place was the modern ball--joint arrangement. Ford came out with ball joints in 1954 and Oldsmobile in 1957.

Oldsmobile and Buick introduced the fully curved windshield in their concept cars in 1953 and in their production cars in 1954.

Automatic transmissions became standard equipment in the 1950s for many car manufacturers. If you wanted a standard transmission, you had to order it special from the factory, and wait.

The transmission selector controls were placed in odd locations. Chrysler products used push button selectors on the dash. Edsel used selectors in the steering wheel hub.

The Edsel had an unusual Dash. Photo by Author

Some Edsel transmission pushbutton controls were located in the steering wheel hub
Photo by Author

The Edsel speedometer is floating in fluid.  Photo by Author

Tailfins were the standard of the day, as the fifties progressed.  This culminated in the late 1950s when the fins became so pointed that there was a danger of being hurt if one was not careful. The Cadillac body comes to mind.  Also, in this timeframe, air conditioning was offered, though this option was expensive, and few buyers opted for it.

GM cars introduced the two-door hardtop in 1950.  Chevrolet, Oldsmobile, Cadillac, Pontiac and Buick car designs were gorgeous. Ford Motor Company was caught unawares and spruced up the Ford and Mercury two door coupe.  On the exterior, there was a vinyl top over the steel roof and decorative hub caps.  Internally there was a fancy steering wheel and lots of chrome trim.  The backlighting for the dash gages was a soft green.  Ford named their cars the Crestliner and Mercury, the Monterey.  Ford Motor Company abandoned these models in 1951, when it came out with its own hardtop models.

One cannot forget the Nash "Bathtub" design. This unibodied car was referred to as the "Airflyte." Nash cars had seats that folded into a bed, going way back in time. In 1949 this arrangement was modified so that fully reclining front seatbacks created a sleeping area entirely within the passenger compartment. In 1950 these reclining seatbacks were given the ability to lock into several intermediate positions. Nash soon called these new seatbacks "Airliner Reclining Seats." Many a father refused to allow his daughter to date a boy driving a Nash with folding seats. These Nash automobiles grouped the engine instruments and speedometer/odometer, not in the dashboard, but on a single pod, mounted on the steering column, in front of the driver.

1951 Nash "Bathtub"[8]

Car paint schemes became bold, with two-tone and even three-tone paint jobs. (Packard comes to mind).

Ford produced a "Retractable" from 1957 through 1959. This was a convertible hardtop that was named the Skyliner. The steel hardtop retracted into the trunk.

In the 1940s and 1950s, cars generally were ordered from the factory. The buyer put a down payment, specified what was wanted, and waited about six weeks for the car to be delivered. That is not to say that cars were not "stuffed" into dealerships on speculation. However, in order to obtain the car with the options wanted, the car had to be ordered.

8

The 1958 Ford Skyliner. Photo by Author

Late in the 1950s, quad headlights started making inroads. Apparently, two headlights weren't sufficient from a styling viewpoint, or there was a push for more lighting, I am not sure which.

By 1950, the gas filler tube no longer protruded through the rear fender on Fords. Rather, there was a sheet metal door covering the filler cap. It got to the point that the filler cap was hidden behind a taillight that pivoted for access on some cars.

Ford stressed safety features in the 1956 models. A deep-dish steering wheel and recessed dash controls were standard. Safety belts, padded dash and padded sun visors were optional for extra cost. However, these safety items were not popular with the buying public.

 ←——— Gas filler tube exposed on 1949 Ford

Gas filler tube behind sheet metal door
On 1950 Ford ——→

## Location of gas cap changed from being exposed on the 1949 Ford to hidden on 1950 Ford

 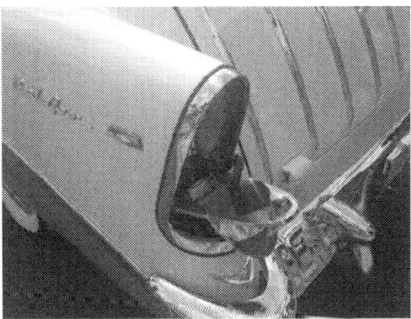

1956 Chevrolet "hidden" gas cap is behlnd taillight
Photo by Author

The 1958 Chevrolet, with quad headlights. Photo by author

1950 Ford Crestliner, a two door coupe spruced up to compete with the GM Hardtops. Photo by author

1950 Mercury Monterey, a two door coupe spruced up to compete with the GM Hardtops. Photo taken by author at the 1986 Early Ford V-8 Eastern National Convention in Westborough, Massachusetts

The 1955 Lincoln made available a powered lubrication system which greased the chassis at the push of a button on the dash. The system was called Multi-Luber[9]. When activated, an electric motor pressurized the system lubricating the chassis, suspension and steering systems.

By the mid-1950s, dash gages were dropped in favor of "idiot" lights. These lights replaced the engine oil pressure, coolant temperature and electrical charging gages. When the engine was operating properly, the lights were not lit. When either the engine oil pressure was too low, the coolant too hot or the generator was discharging, the appropriate "red" light illuminated.

In those days, the life of a car was about 100,000 miles; by then it was about worn out. I blame the engine oil technology, as it did not keep up with the demands of the higher horsepower engines. As far as the car bodies were concerned, after five years of exposure to salt on the roads in the northern tier of states, in winter, rust pretty much consumed the car.

## American Sports Cars

1954 Chevrolet Corvette

1955 Ford Thunderbird

Studebaker Avanti

1954 Kaiser Darrin

American Sports Cars[10]

---

9

10

The mid-fifties saw the introduction of American sports cars. The Corvette was early, in 1954, with its all-fiberglass bodied Corvette. It initially had the Chevrolet six-cylinder engine, but it soon transitioned to the V-8. The car was an instant hit, and continues to have a terrific following today.

Ford countered with the two-seat Thunderbird in 1955. This was an all-steel bodied car, and had an OHV V-8 from its introduction. Kaiser made a limited number of Darrins and Studebaker followed with the Avanti, later on.

<u>Cars had style</u>
Any kid could identify a car make from at least two city blocks away. The following illustration compares a mediocre Chevrolet of 2000 vintage with a 1953 Buick, with the toothy front grill. I used Buick as an example, but I could have used just about any marque.

I was hard pressed to identify the make of the car on the left. I had to walk up to it and observe the emblem. It was a Chevrolet.  In contrast, I could identify the 1953 Buick city blocks ahead.

<u>I especially liked Fords</u>
As I look back to post WWII, Ford came out with its first all-new post-war body style in 1949. When I was a teen, I was crazy about Fords with the flathead V-8 engine; specifically the 1949-1951 Ford and Mercury

When the war ended, Ford went back into civilian production with a warmed over 1942 model; it had a modified grill, some trim changes, but the body style was essentially 1942. The engine was the old tried and true flathead V-8 that was introduced in 1932, but with incremental improvements. It still had the cooling problem that I discuss later, but that was inherent in the basic design.

The Ford drive train was unchanged except for minor improvements. The body retained the kingpin front suspension with a traverse leaf spring, initially introduced on the old Model T. The cars were not equipped with a heater as standard equipment, or a radio. Southern cars didn't need a heater.

1942 Ford Tudor Sedan

This was the last model that was manufactured before production Ceased, in support the war effort

1946 Ford Coupe

This was a warmed over 1942 model, with a new Grill and minor changes

Fords from Pre-War to Post-War[11]

---

[11]

The 1949 Ford Coupe was the first new body style brought out by Ford post WWII. [12]

Fords of this era were the choice of the Hot Rod set, as they had the flathead V-8 engine that could be tricked out with glass-pack mufflers to give a desirable melodious sound. My dream car was a 1950 Ford convertible equipped with dual exhaust and glass pack mufflers, rear wheel skirts, lowered rear suspension and wide whitewall tires. A classmate in engineering school commuted every day from Taunton to Boston, Massachusetts in his 1950 Ford convertible. It was tan colored with a white top. In my freshman year, the car was gorgeous, even though it was seven years old. By the time I graduated, four years later, the car looked pretty ratty. New England winters took its toll.

The car I craved, when in high school, was the 1950 Ford Tudor Coupe with the flathead V-8 engine (not the six-cylinder engine). It had to be painted shiny black and be equipped with wide whitewall (WWW) tires. Of course, the car required rear wheel skirts, painted black to match the body. Dual exhaust with Smithie mufflers and chrome exhaust tips were needed to make that mellow Ford flathead V-8 sound. The rear end needed to be lowered to give the look of motion while the car was still. All this was to be topped off with twin spotlights on either side of the cowl. Alas, I was not able to afford the car of my dreams back then.

Three things were necessary for an engine to run; spark, fuel and compression. Most engine problems were electrical, precluding a spark. Next in the order was the lack of fuel, usually due to a failed fuel pump. Rarely, was engine compression the cause.

In the day, five or six year old cars could be purchased for a price ranging between $175 and $295. American youth grew up working on cars. If a car didn't start, it usually was a simple task to diagnose the problem and have the car on the road quickly. Car-crazy kids visited auto wrecking yards to buy used parts to replace worn engines and transmissions   America's youth grew up working on cars.

Looking back, a ten year span resulted in an incredible improvement in car body style. The collage below depicts the major styling change in Fords from 1930 to 1940, to 1950 and to 1960.

Collage of Ford body styling progressing from 1930 to 1960, in 10 year increments[13]

13

Chapter 2    My First Car; a 1949 Pontiac

As I entered college, I had to have a car. The search began. I commuted to Boston University by bus and train every day. There was a small used-car lot on the bus route, and on that lot was a 1950 Ford four-door sedan. It sported a fire-engine red paint job, had wide whitewall tires, was lowered in the rear, had rear wheel skirts and dual exhaust with glass-pack mufflers. This was a snappy looking car. Each time I passed that car, I became more interested.

Finally, I had to get off the bus, before my stop, and check out this car. The first thing I noticed was that the seat didn't adjust far enough back for my six foot frame. Once the engine was started, there was a grinding noise when I shifted from neutral to first gear. That was a tell-tale sign that the clutch (or transmission) was worn. Also, my arm rested on the window sill, but the sill was so high that it was uncomfortable for me to stay in this position. Unfortunately, this was inherent in the design of the Fords of the period. I reluctantly passed on this car.

1950 Ford Four Door Sedan[14]
This car is similar to the fire engine red-colored car I looked at, but passed on.

My hero, Mother's older brother, Uncle Dave, had a 1949 Pontiac. It was equipped with the straight-eight engine and Hydra-Matic Drive four-speed automatic transmission. Uncle Dave died tragically in 1954, at a young age of 45 years old, from lung cancer. He had been a three-pack-a-day smoker for many years.

I had taken driving school lessons but discontinued them because I was not happy with the instructor, Mr. Cunningham. He was too enamored with himself and spent too much time talking about his motorcycle. I needed to know if I required any more lessons, or if I was ready for my driving test. A neighbor and her young daughter lived across the hall from our apartment. The neighbor worked as a bar maid and hired a nanny to watch her youngster during the day. The nanny had a boyfriend who volunteered to take me out in his car to evaluate my skill. He also had a 1949 Pontiac with the straight-eight engine and Hydra-Matic Drive automatic transmission. After a test ride, he deemed me ready. But first, I needed a car.

It was 1957, and I was in the market for my first car. The Lynn newspaper had an advertisement for a 1950 Ford. When I called, the owner told me that the car had been taken off the road for the winter, but that I could test the clutch in the driveway. He wanted $295 and was not flexible on the price. I didn't have $295 so I passed without looking at it.

I responded to an ad in East Lynn for a 1950 Oldsmobile convertible. I took the bus to look at the car and was disappointed. It was painted white with a white colored top. Both the paint and top were worn and dirty. The car also was rusty. The fact that the car had the six-cylinder engine instead of the overhead valve V-8 was the clincher. I immediately passed on the car.

A used car lot in Saugus had a 1950 Mercury sedan for sale. The salesman couldn't start the engine. He explained that the car had an electric fuel pump, and that was the reason for the malfunction. The rationale didn't make sense to me, and I again passed.

I was in love with the body style of the 1949-1951 Mercury and the melodious sound that came from the flathead engine dual exhaust with glass-pack mufflers. A friendly neighbor was a salesman for a business form company. He had a lead on a 1949 Mercury sedan in a garage in Salem, Massachusetts. The car had been repaired, and had not been picked up. The garage owner told my neighbor that if the car was not recovered by a certain date, I could buy it for the cost of the repairs. I was excited and patiently waited for the expiration date. The next thing I knew, the car went up for a sheriff's auction, but the owner showed up and paid the bill. I guess I never was meant to have that car.

I located a green 1949 Pontiac two-door fastback on the used car lot of Sea Crest Pontiac. It had the straight-eight engine, but with the three-speed standard transmission. When I test drove the car, the transmission gears had an objectionable whine. This was normal for the straight-cut gears extant on standard transmissions of the period. The rear wheels sported snow tires; I assumed that the howl from the rear was due to the tire tread pattern, but it could have been due to a bearing in the rear end. The last item of note was the clutch which chattered when the pedal was let out. The howl in the rear and the chattering clutch should have disqualified this sale, but I was young and stupid. I asked a friend of the family, and owner of a service station, to look at the car for me. He did and said that it looked reasonable for the money. I followed his input and bought the 1949 Pontiac fastback car for $175.

Since I was under-age, the car was titled in Mother's name. After she came home from work, we both walked to the used car lot on the Lynnway, and she filled out the paperwork to purchase the car. I then scheduled my driving test. On the appointed day, Mother and I went to the Massachusetts Division of Motor Vehicles (DMV) for my driving test. I passed with flying colors. The DMV inspector wrote out my "pink slip" (temporary driver's license) and was about to get out of my car, when I asked who I paid my $15 fee to. He was relieved to hear my question, as he forgot to collect the fee and would have had to make up the lost revenue from his own funds.

As soon as I drove the car home, I had to take my friends out for a ride. Mother was nervous, as the car was in her name, but I paid for the car and had to show it off. I picked up my friends and we rode to Richardson's Ice Cream, in Middleton, about five miles away. Upon returning home, Mother was anxious. I told her she could take the car out with her friends. The next day she did. A block from our apartment, the car stalled in traffic, and would not restart. When the engine cooled, it started normally. I didn't know it at the time, but this was a classic case of vapor lock. The under-hood temperatures got hot to the point that the fuel in the tube leading to the fuel pump changed to a vapor state from a liquid state. The mechanical fuel pump was incapable of "sucking" fuel vapor, only liquid fuel. I lived with that situation for the period that I owned the car.

I complained to my friends that the car had no heat, in the winter. I could not feel any hot air coming from under the dash. My assistant manager at Stop & Shop Supermarket pointed out to me that this car had the heater core under the front seat. The fan was integral with the heater core, and when I turned the fan "On" for heat, the warm air came up from under the front seat. Problem solved.

The first week that I owned the car, the battery failed. I called our family friend, and he brought me a new battery on his way home from work. I believe that the battery cost me $15. It was unlike those in use now, in that it was long and narrow. This helped with its fit in the allotted space.

I used the car to commute to college by driving either to the rapid transit (MTA or Metropolitan Transit Authority) station, or driving directly to school, depending on the time of day and the projected availability of parking at school. I liked that Pontiac. It had great low speed torque. I could slow the speed to five miles per hour, in third gear, dump the throttle, and the car nicely picked up speed without complaining.

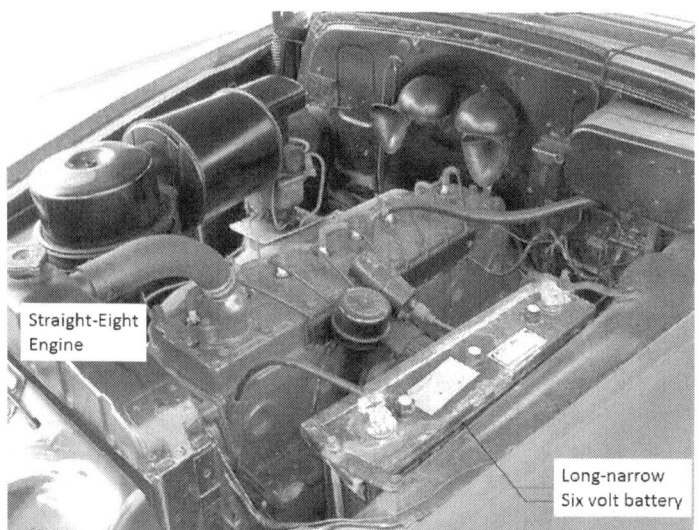

Straight-Eight Engine

Long-narrow Six volt battery

1949 Pontiac Straight Eight Engine; Note the long narrow battery[15]

1949 Pontiac[16]
Note the beautiful lines of the first postwar redesign

Chapter 3     My Second Car; a 1950 Mercury Coupe

It was 1959 and I sold the 1949 Pontiac for $150, for a loss of $25 from the purchase price two years earlier. The search was on. Obey Motors on Commercial St., in Lynn, had a 1950 Mercury Coupe on the lot. I knew instantly that I wanted that car. I should have been suspicious, as it had a safety inspection sticker considerably out of date. In those days, in Massachusetts, cars had to be inspected spring and fall of every year. I took the car for a test drive. As I shifted from first to second gear, the transmission made a slight grinding noise. With all the background that I have now, I know either, or both, the clutch and the transmission synchronizers were shot, but I wanted the car. The radio did not work, nor did the speedometer. The car was "nosed" and "decked," which meant that the previous owner removed the hood and trunk ornaments and filled in the holes with lead and primer paint. As I said, I wanted that car! The price was $295 minus the $150 I had from the sale of my 1949 Pontiac. I paid out the balance owed over the summer from my earnings at the Stop & Shop Supermarket.

1950 Mercury Coupe
This was actually the second Mercury coupe that I owned, in the 1980s. However, my first 1950 Mercury was the same model. Photo by Author

I purchased a pair of rear wheel skirts from a Western Auto store, and painted them with red primer from a paint spray can. In 1958, there was a fire in my apartment house. The fire was actually in the apartment across the hall from us, but the fire department did a good job of hosing down everything. My 1950 Mercury was parked in front of the apartment building and sustained quite a bit of soaking. I submitted a claim to my insurance company for the faded paint on the car. The insurance company paid me $150 to settle the claim. This was enough to paint the car back then; I wanted to paint the car gloss black. I just couldn't pull the trigger to actually paint the car. I used the money for college, which I suppose was the grown-up thing to do.

The grocery manager at Stop & Shop Supermarket, where I worked part time, repaired car radios as a hobby. I pulled the radio out of the car and gave it to him. He got it operating, but said that it looked like it had been sitting in water, and was corroded. The car radio didn't work for very long. I made do without a car radio.

The used car dealer provided the standard 50/50 warranty for 30 days. This meant that the cost of any repair was jacked up by 100%, and the dealer paid 50%. I thought that was fair. NOT! I returned the car to repair the emergency brake cable, which snapped, under warranty. The dealer fixed it, as it was a safety inspection issue. I then returned the car for the grinding in the transmission. The dealer brought the car across the street to a Citgo gas station, and had the mechanic look at it. He said that the clutch was shot and had no adjustment left. The sales manager put on a good act and said, "There had to be (an adjustment), There had to be!" while chain smoking cigarettes. The mechanic put on an act seemingly to adjust the clutch, and I went on my way with nothing resolved.

I commuted to Revere where I boarded the Metropolitan Transit Authority (MTA) train to college. I parked on a side street and endured the mad stares of the residents for daring to park on their street. One day, upon returning, the car would not start. I got a push for a couple of city blocks to a Gulf service station, and left the car to be repaired.

Upon returning to pick up the car, the mechanic told me that the fuel pump had failed and it was replaced. When I started the car, the fuel pump made a sound like, "Whump, Whump Whump."

I needed to report to work in Salem, so I paid the bill and drove off. Several miles away, the car broke down. The ignition rotor was cracked. Somehow I had the rotor replaced and went on my way. Later I broke down again, for the same reason. Apparently there was a tiny clip inside the ignition rotor that prevented it from orbiting as it rotated, and it was missing. The service shop in Revere that replaced the fuel pump must have cannibalized the part for another car! As I wrote this section, it occurred to me that perhaps someone in the neighborhood where I parked the car stole the clip out of spite. And, maybe the service station simply replaced the fuel pump to make money. I will never know.

When in my junior year in college, I took the car to McManus Garage in Lynn to look at the grinding noise. The mechanic told me that the clutch was the problem. I used the $50 the Air Force ROTC Advanced Corps paid me every quarter to pay for the clutch replacement. While driving away from the garage, the transmission made the same noise. I brought it back and the mechanic now said that the transmission was bad. I had no more money, so I continued to drive the car with the grinding between first and second gear.

One night, after working at Stop & Shop Supermarket, I drove home. It was winter and freezing rain was falling like dew. It was obvious that the road was slippery, and I drove carefully and slow. Several blocks from home, on a secondary road with a stop sign at the end, I attempted to stop the car. I knew it was slippery, so, at a crawl, I depressed the clutch in anticipation of stopping at the sign. As soon as the brakes were gingerly applied, the car swapped the front end for the rear end. The car made a slow 180 degree turn in the middle of the road. I was lucky as I did not hit anything; the car just stopped facing the other direction. There were no other cars on the road. That was an experience!

In 1960, after graduating from college, I took the car off the road. It sat in the yard to the rear of our apartment building. I did not have confidence to drive the car from Lynn, Massachusetts to Waco, Texas, and then drive it every day in local use. Close to my date to report to the Air Force, I sold the car for $150, for a loss of $145 off the purchase price.

There was a problem; the passenger-side front tire was flat. Also, the front bumper was missing a bolt on that side, so when the front bumper was jacked up, it twisted badly. Somehow, I managed to change the tire. It was funny; back then I had absolutely no mechanical ability whatsoever. All that was necessary was to buy a bolt, nut and washer from an auto parts store and secure the bumper to the frame. Later in life, I would view engineers who couldn't do that simple a job, with contempt.

Flathead V-8 Engine in the 1950 Mercury[17]

---

Chapter 4    Characteristics of Cars in the 1950s

Looking back, the technology built into cars and the experience of driving cars in that era was markedly different than today, as I discuss below.

Tires:   Cars utilized bias-ply tires which tended to take a set, when parked overnight.  In the morning, the tires had a slight flat spot where they were in contact with the ground.  There was a thumping sound when the car was initially driven, until the tire completely rounded out after a few miles.  Also, bias-ply tires had a tendency to follow every slight dip in the road surface.  The driver was constantly correcting the steering.  The next time the reader watches an old movie of the period, and there is a driving scene, note that the driver constantly corrects the steering.  After driving for a while, without power steering, the driver's arms become tired.

Tires came with inner tubes, and whitewall tires, if one wanted to spend the extra money.  Many people did not purchase whitewalls, as money was tight.  Less expensive was the port-o-wall whitewall insert.  This was a fake whitewall that was inserted to the outside of the tire to make it look like a whitewall tire.  Tubeless tires made their introduction in the mid-1950s.

Tire technology has come a long way.  In the fifties, having a flat tire was quite common.  Today, I cannot remember when I had a flat tire on my modern car.

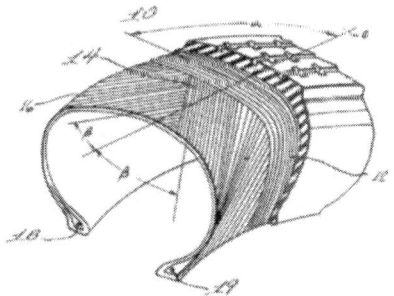

In a radial tire, the plies are oriented as depicted by "12."
In a bias ply tire, the plies are oriented as depicted by "14 and 16."[18]

---

18

Engine Oil;    Engine oil was not up to the standards of today. The oil companies transitioned from single grade 30-weight non-detergent oil to multi-grade oil, such as 10W-30. The engine horsepower was increasing, as the fifties progressed, but the oil technology wasn't keeping pace. For example, when Oldsmobile introduced the modern overhead valve 303 cubic inch V-8 engine in 1949, the valve lifters were hydraulically actuated. When the engine started, oil pressure took up the cold clearance in the valve train. The theory was good, but the oil tended to degrade and the tiny clearances in the hydraulic lifters became clogged with coked oil. The result was a pronounced "ticking" sound from the engine that was proportional to engine speed (RPM). The solution was to replace the valve lifter. It was common to hear Oldsmobiles "ticking" while operating.

Another example was the flathead Ford engine. It had a tendency to run hot. The result was the oil tended to coke, or become solidified. When these engines were torn town for rebuild, it was common to scoop out the coked oil, or sludge, with a spoon, from the oil pan.

Engine oil filters were not standard. In the immediate pre-war period, an oil filter was an accessory, available at extra cost. Further, the oil filter was not a full-flow filter that is standard on cars today. Rather, the filter was a bypass type. The oil pump discharge was split. A portion of the discharge was diverted through the bypass oil filter and then on to the engine. The balance was routed directly to the engine for lubrication. Today, the full-flow units filter 100% of the oil pump discharge before the oil is routed to the engine for lubrication.

Cars of that era all leaked or burned oil. As far as oil leakage was concerned, the seal and gasket materials in the engine, transmission and rear end (the drive train) were not as good as those available today. It was common to see ugly black spots, from oil leakage, on the driveway under where cars were parked. As far as oil burning was concerned, the quality of the oils used and poor attention to regular oil change intervals resulted in contaminants accumulating in the engine.

This caused wear and increased clearances between moving and static parts, thereby allowing oil to bypass the piston rings and burn in the combustion chambers. My friend, and retired mechanic, lamented, "All old cars leaked oil. That was not worrisome. Once the leak stopped, it was time to worry, because then the car was out of oil."

The engine crankcase was vented to atmosphere. When the car was parked, there was the residual odor of oil mist coming out of the breather on top of the engine. The pumping action of the pistons churned up the oil. If there was nowhere for the oil mist to go, it would tend to pressurize the crankcase. To relieve this pressure, an oil vent (breather) was added. Furthermore, if the piston rings were worn, then the crankcase would tend to pressurize from the blow-by past the pistons and there would be significant oil mist purged out of the engine through the breather. In any event, there was always an oil mist smell coming from the oil breather.

Chassis Lubrication: There were tens of grease fittings in the chassis. Fittings were on the upper and lower kingpins, on both sides, steering pivot points, universal joint, driveshaft, clutch pivot points, and rear wheel bearings. It was common for the factory to recommend an oil change and chassis lubrication every 2000 miles. That might have been respectable back then, but today, with the average mileage driven between 15,000 to 20,000 miles per year, the lubrication requirement would be burdensome.

Steering: Power steering was offered only on upscale cars. With manual steering, when the car was stationary, it was difficult to turn the wheel, as when parking. A slight movement of the car made turning the wheel easier.

Headlights: The six-volt headlight bulbs were weak. Until about 1939, there was a reflector behind the bulb, but over time, the silver in the coating would tarnish and the bulb lighting dimmed. My opinion of the headlights was that they barely showed other cars that you were there, as opposed to actually lighting up the road in front of the car. In 1940, Ford abandoned the take-apart headlight, and incorporated the sealed beam headlight. Late in the 1950s, Quad headlights replaced the dual headlight designs.

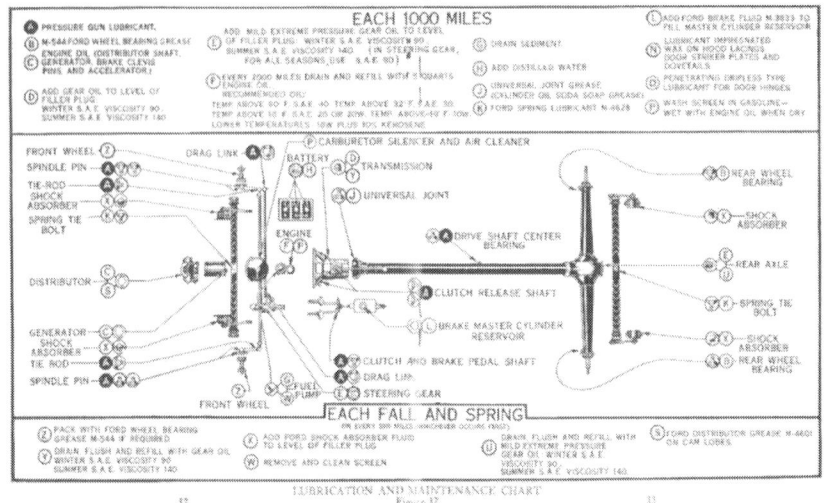

Early Ford Lubrication Chart[19]
Extract from the Ford Passenger and Commercial Reference Book 1939

Brakes: Many manufacturers introduced hydraulically actuated brakes early in the 1930s. Ford was among the last holdouts, finally offering hydraulic brakes in 1939. The stopping distance was somewhat improved over mechanical braking systems. Also, each wheel brake had a Coarse and a Fine mechanical setting that had to be adjusted periodically. Self-adjusting brakes came into vogue later. As the fifties progressed, power braking systems came common, and stopping distances were greatly reduced.

Hill Holder[20]       The hill-holder function worked by using two sensors, in concert with the brake system on the vehicle. The first sensor measured the forward-facing incline (nose higher than tail) of the vehicle, while the second was a disengaging mechanism.

The 1930s-1950s NoRoL used a ball bearing as a check valve in the hydraulic brake line; when the car was on an uphill incline, the ball rolled back and blocked the brake line; When the car was level or facing downhill, the ball rolled away, leaving the line free. The clutch linkage slightly dislodged the ball when the clutch was released, enabling the car to move away from a stop. When the car was level or facing downhill, the ball rolled away, leaving the line free.

Once set, the driver had to keep the clutch pedal fully depressed but could remove the foot from the brake pedal. To disengage the system and move the car forward, the driver selected first gear, gently depressed the fuel pedal, and slowly released the clutch pedal, which, at a point in its travel, released the brake system. This allowed the car to proceed.

Although Studebaker introduced the system in the 1930s, a hill holder could be purchased from a parts store from the 1930s through the 1950s, for retrofit. However, the car had to have hydraulic brakes, so the earliest a Ford could retrofit the system was 1939 on, when Ford introduced hydraulic brakes.

Engine cooling:    As I have stated many times, the Ford flathead engine had an inherent defect; it ran hot. The reason was the engine exhaust gas was routed internally through cored passages in the intake manifold to preheat the intake mixture of fuel and air. This additional heat load made cooling more difficult. As I experienced with my 1939 Ford, I was particularly wary of traffic tie-ups. The engine coolant temperature would start to soar in no time flat when stuck in traffic. One trick was to run the passenger compartment heater, as it was an additional radiator. On a hot summer day, this didn't do much for cabin comfort, but it helped cool the engine. Other car manufacturers did not have the problem that was extant on Fords. The cooling system was atmospheric, which meant that it was vented to atmosphere; there was no pressure in the system. As the fifties progressed, pressurized cooling systems came along to raise the boiling point of the coolant.

My mechanic friend stated that the flathead Ford V-8 ran at a temperature of ambient plus 100F. So, if the outside air was 85 degrees F, the flathead ran at 185 degrees. Of course, it depended on whether the car was operating normally, at speed. Idling in traffic, the temperature soared.

In those days, the radiators used either a water/alcohol mixture or "permanent antifreeze." The alcohol in the mix was volatile, and it tended to boil off. At a gasoline service station, the service attendant tested the coolant freeze point to make sure that there was sufficient alcohol in the radiator. Permanent antifreeze was more expensive, so more people used the water/alcohol mixture.

Windshield Wipers: The windshield wipers were actuated using engine vacuum. When the car climbed a hill, the engine developed low vacuum, and the wiper blades stalled or actuated very slowly. Going downhill was the opposite; the engine developed high vacuum, and the blades slapped back and forth furiously.

Along came the double-acting fuel pump. One chamber of the fuel pump moved a diaphragm up and down, sucking and pushing the fuel from the fuel tank to the carburetor. The other chamber developed a vacuum that assisted the engine vacuum in operating the windshield wipers. When it operated as advertised, the double acting fuel pump made the windshield wipers less dependent on engine vacuum, alone, and helped even out the back and forth strokes of the blades.

Visibility: Pre-war and immediately post-war, visibility to the rear was poor, especially in the convertible, as the rear window was small. Visibility improved with later models.

Paint: The cars were painted using Nitrocellulose Lacquer. It was easy to spray without expensive equipment, and could be spot painted to touch-up spots. This paint was "soft" and would chip easily. However, currently, the Environmental Protection Agency (EPA) has banned this paint because of its volatility. It is still available to hobbyists, but professional shops will not use it as the EPA could shut them down. Modern paints mixed to give the same color are preferred, today.

1939 Ford Convertible Coupe rear glass afforded poor visibility to the rear of the car.
Photo by Author

Radio:      The sound from the radio was "tinny." The radio was powered by vacuum tubes that consumed a moderate amount of electrical power. Operating the radio without the engine running for more than about 15 minutes could result in the drawdown of the battery and an inability to start the engine. So, when "parking" with your honey, watching the "Submarine Races," you had to be careful about keeping the radio operating for any length of time.

We didn't have the "Instant-On" feature in radios of the era. After turning the radio "On," there was a wait time while the vacuum tubes warmed up. This took approximately ten to 15 seconds.

There was only the AM radio band, with no feature to play recorded music, as on eight track or cassette tapes,

Exhaust      Hot Rodders retrofitted glass-pack mufflers on the V-8 engines in order to get that throaty sound. Also, a dual-exhaust system was retrofitted in order to look "cool," and "duals" also reduced the back pressure on the engine, enabling it to develop a small amount of added power. The local law enforcement officials were on the lookout for the cars with loud noise. One trick of the day was to stuff steel wool in the tail pipe to quiet down the engine exhaust, when necessary.

The exhaust systems were made of steel with poor anti-corrosion characteristics. A couple of winters with exposure to salt on the roads and the exhaust system corroded through and had to be replaced. The muffler shops did a good business in the rust belt of the country. Of course, today, stainless steel exhaust systems last the life of the car.

<u>Cool Stuff Hanging from the Rear View Mirror</u>     Hot     Rodders had to have a shrunken head dangling from the rear view mirror. Some had oversized fuzzy dice, others had their high school graduation tassel, but I preferred the shrunken head. I was stopped by an unmarked Registry of Motor Vehicles car while commuting home from college. The official made me remove the shrunken head, because it "obstructed my vision."

<u>Curb feelers</u>    We also had curb feelers. These mounted on the front fenders and would scrape the curb when we parked the car before the fender scraped.

Curb Feeler in front of right front wheel of a 1953 De Soto    Car owned by Alan Stone, President of The Villages, Florida AACA. Photo by Author

Rear Wheel Skirts     The car <u>had</u> to have rear wheel skirts in order to look cool.

Rear Wheel Skirts displayed on my 1956 Oldsmobile Starfire.  Photo by Author

## Dressed-up Hub Caps

Hot Rodders had to have fancy hubcaps.  My favorite was the spinner hubcap that was an option for the Oldsmobile.  These hubcaps were subsequently put on many other cars, such as Ford, Mercury, and Cadillac among others.

Spinner hubcap installed on my 1956 Oldsmobile Starfire
Photo by Author

<u>Suicide Knob</u> The "Suicide Knob" bolted to the steering wheel and allowed the car to be steered using one hand. They were also known as "Necker Knobs" because they allowed the driver to have one hand free to engage his female companion. One had to be careful when cornering in a car without power steering, as the wheel had the natural tendency to rapidly straighten coming out of the curve; and the knob could injure the driver's hand.

<u>Odors from old cars</u>
Remember the odors from old cars? The upholstery was made from broadcloth, mohair or Bedford cord. Over time, the upholstery tended to emit a unique if musty odor.

Engines had a crankcase oil vent, as described above. On top of this vent tube was a cap with a steel mesh, whose function was to allow the air to escape and condense the oil mist, which in turn dripped back into the engine oil pan.

Whenever a car engine was shut down, there was a lingering odor of oil around the engine. The oil mist trap was not 100% efficient, so a small amount of oil or mist escaped into the atmosphere, causing the odor.

Crankcase Oil Vent with Cap

"Suicide Knob" installed on my 1956 Oldsmobile Starfire
Photo by Author

Continental Kit     A popular accessory was the continental kit. This was an extension of the rear bumper and incorporated a spare tire holder.  It not only looked cool, but it opened up space in the trunk where the spare tire would have been stored.

Typical Continental Kit; photo by author

Blue-Dot Tail Lights
Red brake-light lenses could be purchased with a blue-dot jewel in the center.  When the brakes were actuated, the brake light emitted a purple glow.  This looked cool but was illegal.  Local police departments frowned upon blue-dot tail lights

Another cool accessory was the front windshield sun visor.

Front windshield sun visor.  Photo by Author

GM Autronic Eye mounted on dash.  Photo by Author

Autronic Eye[21]

In 1952, Oldsmobile and Cadillac offered an Autronic Eye, the first automatic headlight-dimming system. When the phototube mounted on the dashboard detected approaching headlights, it would automatically switch the car's beams to low until the other lane was clear. This device eliminated the need for the driver to switch back and forth between low and high beam while driving at night. Other manufacturers, such as Chrysler, had their own version of an automatic headlight dimmer.

Electrical Systems;     Auto electrical systems transitioned from six to 12 volt systems. Ford had a confusing "positive" ground as opposed to many other makes that used negative ground. Pontiac had a long narrow battery developing six volts. Only a few suppliers make an authentic battery for antique cars, today. They ship the battery dry, for safety, and the buyer must purchase sulfuric acid at an auto parts store to activate the battery.

In the winter, trying to start a car in the cold after it was sitting overnight usually was no problem. However, if the car didn't start after the first few tries, the battery usually didn't have enough juice to continue turning the starter motor. The six volt systems had only so much reserve, especially with the higher horsepower engines that were making their way into production.

Traction in winter;     Chains were the option of choice on the drive wheels in the rear, when the weather was icy. When one link of a chain came loose, the turning rear wheel would beat the dickens out of the sheet metal wheel well.

---

21

Tire Chains[22]

Later, studded snow tires became the vogue. That is, until the local highway departments realized that the studs were taking their toll on the road surface. Then, studded snow tires were allowed only in winter. Later, all-season tires replaced the studded snow tires.

Another option was the lighted fender marker. This allowed the driver to see the physical limits of the fenders.

Lighted Fender "Marker"
Photo by Author

Full Service Gas Stations;   All service stations were manned by service attendants.  He/she filled the gas, checked the oil level, cleaned the windshield, checked the tire air pressure, checked the water level in the battery and serviced the cooling system.  Cars of the period eventually burned oil, as it was not what it is today.  Worn piston rings and valves allowed oil to seep into the cylinders and be burned.  Slick service station attendants shoved the oil dipstick only partway into the oil tube, so it would show the need for a quart of oil.  They sold a lot more oil that way.

Every service station had a rack full of free maps.  That was the way the oil companies encouraged touring, and the purchase of gasoline.  It was rumored, in order to keep tabs on bogus maps, each oil company planted a non-existent town on the display.  I don't know if that was true.

Tune-ups;   Cars needed a tune-up every 10,000 miles.  This required replacement of the spark plugs, ignition points, rotor and condenser, sometimes ignition wires, distributor cap, adjustment of the ignition timing and a carburetor adjustment.  Today's cars are fairly immune to tune-ups and frequently go 100,000 miles with only changing the oil, filters and rotating the tires.

Transmissions;   Most cars of the early 1950s had standard shift.  As the decade moved along, automatic transmissions became more prevalent.  In Massachusetts, one could obtain a driver's license for an automatic transmission-powered car, only.  My wife had one when we were married.  When we moved to Texas, and I bought a new 1961 Volkswagen with standard shift, she had to learn the standard.  She took to it quickly, and was proficient by the time we moved back to Massachusetts.

Columbia Two-Speed Rear End for Ford Products
The Columbia two-speed rear axle offered a low gear ratio for low-speed pulling power and fast acceleration from a dead stop. It could then be shifted into a higher ratio on the fly to give the vehicle a smoother and more efficient ride for highway speeds. The higher ratio also allowed the engine to run at a lower rpm once the car was moving fast enough to utilize the second speed or ratio.

Normal operation of the overdrive unit involved getting the car up to speed in 3rd gear, then depressing the clutch pedal and pulling on the overdrive cable. After hearing a solid clunk (telling you the overdrive's been activated), you release the clutch and you're in overdrive. The second speed reduced the axles' original ratio, resulting in a 30% reduction in engine rpm. Although intended for highway speeds, you could engage the overdrive in 1st or 2nd as well; it actually worked in any forward gear. The Columbia unit could be found in Ford products up to 1948.

If you can find a Ford product with this overdrive unit operational, it is a real find. Over the years, when Fords were junked, many wrecking yards saved Columbia Two-Speed units, but scrapped the controls which were mounted on the dash.

### Borg- Warner Overdrive Transmissions

In 1949, Ford offered the Borg-Warner Overdrive for an extra $97. This overdrive was an electrically actuated Borg-Warner planetary gearbox residing directly behind the three-speed transmission. At a car speed of 60 mph, Overdrive gearing gave engine speed of only 42 mph. Noted one ad, "It accents the new Ford 'Feel' while it saves you gas, saves your oil and saves your engine!"

As the Ford advertisement went on to describe Overdrive operation, in rather exclamatory style: "Let up on the gas pedal above 27 miles per hour and a miracle happens! You're in fourth gear for cruising! Engine speed drops 30% while the car speed remains unchanged! The Ford Overdrive seems to give your car wings, it's so smooth, so quiet and so free of vibration!"

The Overdrive kick down switch was beneath the gas pedal. As the Ford ad continued, "And should you require a burst of extra power, simply press through on the accelerator and you return to conventional third gear. It was just as simple as that!"

There were technical aspects as well: "You'll call it a 'tip-toe miracle.' Engineers call it a 'simple automatic planetary transmission, combined with the regular three-speed transmission as a single unit.' "

Gasoline;    Gasoline was cheap. I recall $.22/gallon. I got together with the guys and we pooled our resources. For a dollar, we could drive all evening.

### Oil Bath Air Cleaner[23]

The oil bath air cleaner consisted of a sump containing a shallow pool of oil, and an insert which is filled with a mesh coarse filter media. When the cleaner is assembled, the media-containing body of the insert sits a short distance above the surface of the oil pool. The rim of the insert overlaps the rim of the sump.

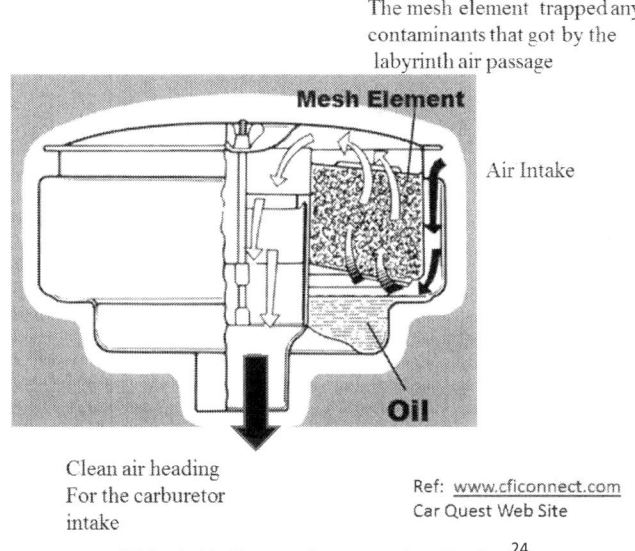

The mesh element trapped any contaminants that got by the labyrinth air passage

Mesh Element

Air Intake

Oil

Clean air heading
For the carburetor
intake

Ref: www.cficonnect.com
Car Quest Web Site

Oil Bath Air Cleaner Cross-section, Typical[24]

This arrangement forms a labyrinthine path through which the air must travel in a series of U-turns: up through the gap between the rims of the insert and the sump, down through the gap between the outer wall of the insert and the inner wall of the sump, and up through the filter media in the body of the insert. This U-turn takes the air at high velocity across the surface of the oil pool. Larger and heavier dust and dirt particles in the air cannot make the turn due to their inertia, so they fall into the oil and settle to the bottom of the base bowl. Lighter and smaller particles are trapped by the filtration media in the insert, which is wetted by oil droplets aspirated there by normal airflow.

Oil Bath Air Cleaner viewed on my 1956 Oldsmobile.  Photo by Author

Massachusetts Safety Inspections;  Safety Inspections were required twice a year, in the spring and fall.  The inspections were for safety items only, such as operational headlights, brake lights and so forth. A unique colored inspection sticker was applied to the upper part of the windshield, just under the rear view mirror, to signify that the car passed the inspection.  There was no emissions test at that time.  Can you imagine having to schedule a safety inspection twice a year today?

Massachusetts Safety Inspection Sticker.
Spring and fall the car had to be inspected. The sticker
changed colors with each inspection. Photo by Author

Registration;          The Massachusetts car registration expired on
December 31 of each year. New license plates were stamped at the
state prisons; each year plate had a different color, so your car stood
out with an expired license plate. By December 31, the bolts and
nuts securing the license plate to the car were corroded from the
winter roadway salt, and the breakaway torque to remove them was
high. Frequently, the bolts simply snapped off, or the slotted head
deformed and the bolt had to be drilled out. Many a car owner could
be seen struggling with a screw driver on the last day of the year,
with frozen hands, swearing a blue streak, while attempting to
remove the license plate bolts.

New Car Quality;      Mass production allowed new car prices to
remain reasonable. However, in the 1950s, this same mass
production resulted in mediocre quality. When a new car was
purchased and was about to be driven off the dealer's lot, the parting
conversation revolved around the new owner making a list of items
to be adjusted or repaired. It was then necessary to make an
appointment in about two weeks to take care of the "list." The fit
and finish of new cars of the era was just not up to the standard of
today. The new car warranty reflected that quality. A typical car
manufacturer's warranty was 60 days or six thousand miles,
whichever came first. The manufacturer didn't want to be
responsible for the new car for too long.

Impressed with Car Designs of the Mid-1950s
In the summer of 1959, I received orders to attend the Air Force
Reserve Officers' Training Corps summer camp at Lockbourne Air
Force Base, outside Columbus, Ohio.

This was a required four-week training encampment in order to be commissioned a 2$^{nd}$ Lieutenant upon college graduation. A group of Boston University cadets drove out in two cars, a 1951 Chevrolet and a 1953 Mercury sedan. We were allowed to go off-base on one weekend. A couple of us thumbed a ride. An enlisted man stopped to give us a lift in his 1955 Ford Convertible. It was a stunning car, with standard shift and glass-pack mufflers. I was so impressed with the melodious sound from the exhaust that I vowed to buy a similar car someday.

During my college years, 1957 through 1960, car designs evolved to the point of being unattractive to me. I loved the designs of the 1955 and 1956 models, but starting in 1957, the designs turned me off. By the time I graduated college, married and entered the Air Force, in 1961, the looks of new cars disillusioned me. Just after marriage, I reported to the Air Force Undergraduate Navigator School in Waco, Texas, and had to buy a car. As I still had the Fords of 1955 and 1956 on my brain, I found a 1955 Ford Crown Victoria on a used car lot. The garage located on the entry road to James Connolly Air Force Base was operated by a retired Air Force mechanic. He checked out the Ford and told me not to buy it. I wanted it, and bought it anyway.

The mechanic was right, and I traded the car for a used 1956 Chevrolet four-door sedan at a Chevrolet dealer. This car used too much oil, so I took it back to the same garage on the entry road to the base. The mechanic tore down the engine and replaced the piston rings. That solved the oil consumption problem.

A few months later, I anticipated assignment, after graduating navigator school, to the Radar Bombardier School at Mather AFB, Sacramento, California. I thought it would be a good idea to purchase a car with better gas mileage. One Saturday, Marilyn and I drove to Dallas, a 90 mile trip, and traded the Chevrolet for a new 1961 Volkswagen Beetle. I owned that car for the next four years, although not assigned to schooling at Mather AFB, but rather to an operational assignment at Otis AFB, Cape Cod in KC-97 tankers.

Our first new car; a 1961 Volkswagen Beetle purchased in Waco, Texas. The car was equipped with an air-cooled 40 hp engine with four speed manual transmission. Photo by Author

No radio, no gas gauge; Price $1667

My wife, Marilyn, is posing in front of our 1956 Chevrolet four door sedan.

Jefferson Apartments, 1107 Jefferson Ave., Waco, Texas, Spring 1961

Chapter 5     Latent Interest in Antique Cars Awakened

The story forwards to 1979, when I was 40 years old.  A friend was responsible for me being in the old-car hobby.  I knew him from GE, where I worked.  We both attended a week-long seminar off-site in "Interpersonal Awareness."  He took his 1948 Chrysler to class one day and I was hooked.

One exercise in particular stuck with me.  We each had a journal in which we entered any information we wanted.  The moderator had us select a new page, and draw a line across the top of the page.  Then we put tick marks, starting from the left, with our date of birth, today's date in the middle, and on the right, our day of death.  During this time, there was mood music playing from a tape recorder.  Wow, this was getting heavy.  Under the line we listed all the things we wanted to do in our life that we had not accomplished.  Today, we would call this our bucket list.  Next to each item we wrote what was preventing us from accomplishing the desired item.  I suddenly realized that I wanted to restore an antique car.  This exercise plus exposure to the 1948 Chrysler brought that desire from my subconscious into my conscious.

I was a mechanical design engineer at the GE Small Jet Engine Division.   My job required skills using wrenches, as I was responsible for the external configuration of the J85 turbojet engine.  Each redesign required a prototype part be fabricated and assembled to our full size engine mockup.  Over time, I concluded that working on a car was no different than working on a jet engine, in terms of the skills necessary for assembly and disassembly.  I started working on my everyday car in earnest, along with my teen-aged son, Scott.  We developed skills that stayed with us ever since.  I felt that we could handle routine assembly and disassembly of an antique car.

## The Search for a Project Car

My two sons were in their senior year in high school, and college was coming up fast. I never did anything for myself, and I decided that I was going to restore an antique car, in spite of the looming college expenses. I started searching the antique car section of the local *Want Ad* book. I was particularly interested in a Ford or Mercury of 1950s vintage, because I remembered the melodious exhaust sound, with dual exhaust and glass pack mufflers.

## My Advice;  Decision Point; Restore a Car or Buy Restored

Once I was hooked on owning an antique car, the first decision to be made was whether to restore a car or buy one already restored.

## Argument in Favor of Buying a Restored Car

The major advantage to buying a restored car is that the cost is less than the cost to actually restore a car. There are exceptions, of course, especially when considering the restoration of an expensive classic car, such as a Duesenberg. The condition of the restoration can be evaluated before purchase; the best way to do this is to have the car professionally appraised. If the car of interest is out of state, there are professional appraisers who will do the job, and it is well worth the cost, even if the car is not purchased.

## Argument in Favor of Restoring an Antique Car

The advantage of restoring a car is that you will know every nut and bolt on the car by the time it is finished. You will meet many interesting people and have the knowledge that you accomplished a major task. However, you must be practical, in that some restoration tasks are better left to a professional. And that is all right!

For instance, the engine rebuild requires special tooling and expertise that is available at an engine machine shop. Also, unless you are proficient at body work, this task is better left to professionals. Paints used today can lead to cancer; painting a car without the proper breathing protection can kill you. So, in most cases, you will not be able to accomplish the complete restoration yourself, unless you are proficient in all automobile trades. Do what you can and leave the rest to professionals.

## The Specific Make of Car to be Purchased

This is an important decision. If you are nostalgic for a 1948 Pontiac that was your first car as a teen, and you are going to restore one to have forever, then by all means go ahead. However, the cost of restoration will be no different than for a car with a greater following, such as a 1950 Oldsmobile with the "hot" overhead valve 303 cubic inch V-8 and Hydra-Matic Drive transmission. From a financial viewpoint, the 1950 Oldsmobile will be a better investment.

1948 Pontiac Streamliner Deluxe[25]

## Show Car vs. Driver

If the decision is to restore an old car, you must decide what the degree of restoration will be; show car or driver quality.

## Show-Car Quality

Show-car quality requires an enormous outlay of money, because no defect can be tolerated. For example, after sandblasting the frame, a show car will have to have all the former rust pits filled-in and ground-flush, before priming and painting.

The owner of a show-car stores the car in a climate controlled garage, with a dust cover applied. The day of a car show, the car is driven onto an enclosed trailer and towed to the show. Then the car is driven off the trailer, to be displayed and judged. The objective is to win a trophy. After the show, the reverse procedure is followed. Driving the car on the road can reduce the show-car quality appearance quickly, and the investment is too great to allow that.

Driver-Car Quality
Under this level of restoration, the car will look just fine; it might not be perfect, but you will feel comfortable driving it without worrying about every nick and small dent. Driver-quality would entail sandblasting the frame, and applying a primer and top coat paint application. The former rust pits would still be there. Driver-quality is a more practical decision; the restoration will look just fine, but it will not be perfect. The driver-quality car can be driven in antique car tours, cruise-ins and shows. In other words, the driver can be driven and enjoyed.

The Search for the "Right" Car
When searching for an antique car to restore, you should attempt to purchase one from a rust-free area of the country, such as the south, mid-western or western states. Make sure that the car has spent its entire life in that area. Also, insure that the car is complete, without missing parts. You do not want to spend hours freeing up rusted parts and snapping rusted bolts and nuts. An incomplete orphan car (Duesenberg, for example) will present challenges to locate the missing parts, and they will be expensive if and when located. Cars with wide appeal have a large used-part base, both original and reproduction. Fords and Chevrolets come to mind.

Cars that are put up for sale usually are rated by the owner as to condition, using a numbered scale. I have simplified the scale for purposes of this book. Other expanded scales are in use in the hobby. Number One refers to a car whose condition is just as it rolled off the production line. It usually is a car that has just undergone a complete restoration. There are few truly Number One cars, even when they are advertised as such. Again, a professional appraiser should be relied upon to verify the condition.

Most cars that are advertised as Number One are really Number Two. These are cars that are very nice drivers that need little to upgrade to Number One Condition. Number Three cars generally need considerable work, and Number Four cars need total restoration. There are publications that list average antique car auction prices for cars of various conditions. These values need to be taken with a grain of salt, as there are other factors that need to be taken into consideration. Foremost is the strong desire of a potential buyer to actually buy <u>that</u> specific car.

A friend told me a story about the sale of his Ford Model T Roadster. He listed the car for sale at a fair price for the market. There was no response to the ad, and his wife badgered him that his price was too high. After a while, he reduced the price and located a buyer. After the conclusion of the sale, the buyer asked, "Now that I own the car, tell me, why did you sell the car so cheap?" My friend turned to his wife and told her, "See, it's not the price. I needed to find the one person who wanted this specific car."

I started looking for an antique car to restore. I spotted a fire-engine red 1950 Ford convertible for sale on the auto body shop lot across the street from where I worked, at GE. A draftsman friend at work was restoring a Ford Model A, and he advised me not to buy the 1950 Ford convertible because it had a vinyl top instead of the authentic canvas top. This car was driver ready, and that was another reason I passed. I wanted to restore a car rather than simply buy it. That was a big mistake on my part. I don't remember what the price was, but I am sure I spent more on the restoration of the car I eventually bought, a 1939 Ford Convertible Coupe Deluxe.

1950 Ford Convertible in show condition, similar to the one I passed on.
Photo by Author

Also, a 1950 Mercury convertible was for sale on the auto body shop lot. The car was in sorry shape, and needed total restoration. I was told it was on the lot "on consignment." I contacted the owner and took a test ride. The car was truly shot. The lower rocker panels were so rusted that they effectively were missing. One of the two water pumps leaked so badly that there was steam all over the engine compartment. This was the car I should have bought. I believe the price was $3000, as is. I probably could have negotiated a lower price. Restored, this model is collectible today and is worth as much as the car I eventually bought.

On my commute home from work, I passed the Golden Banana, a local strip club. On the front of the parking lot were the remains of a 1951 Mercury Convertible. I saw that car every day, but never stopped to look at it, as it was incomplete; there were many parts missing.

The local Want Advertiser listed a 1940 LaSalle Coupe for sale in Chelsea, behind a gas station. When I looked at the car, it was obvious that it had been in a collision. This car was unusual in that it had shutters behind the radiator to control the cooling airflow. The shutters looked like venetian blinds and were controlled by a thermostatic switch. The car had the Cadillac flathead V-8 engine. This was another car that I passed on, but that I later regretted losing.

1938 LaSalle Series 50[26]

26

Chapter 6     The Find; a 1939 Ford of Danish Heritage

A friend at work told me of a general contractor in Lynn, Massachusetts, who had a 1939 Ford convertible for sale, needing total restoration. I arranged to look at the car. It actually was a collection of rotted-out parts that were stored in two rented garages. I fell in love with a postcard photograph of what the car would look like after restoration. Another item interested me. The car was as old as I was. We were both born in 1939!

I purchased the collection of parts representing the car. The seller purchased it from a former G.I. on Cape Cod. The prior history of the car was unknown. The seller had driven from Lynn, used his torch to take apart the car and load the parts onto his dump truck. (He was a contractor.) He then rented two garages in Lynn where he stored the parts. It was obvious that he wasn't going to restore the car anytime soon, and the garage owners wanted the rental units back. He sold me the car for what he paid. (He said.) I paid him $1500 in 1979. He told me that even if I didn't restore the car, I would get my money back by selling the convertible top bows, alone. He was probably correct.

Picture postcard of the 1939 Ford Convertible Coupe Deluxe, the model that I fell in love with

This car was unique, in that it had been assembled in the Ford plant in Copenhagen, Denmark. Ford had an assembly plant there for many years, and produced Fords for the Scandinavian market.

Danish Ford Heritage

Among the unique features of this car was an export data plate. This was loose, along with most other parts of the car. I just didn't know where it had been mounted. Later, I communicated with a member of the Early Ford V-8 Club, in Sweden, and learned that the export tag was riveted to the floor, under the floor mat on the driver's side. I still have that tag, but have not restored it. I figured that if the plate was covered by the floor mat, it wasn't worth spending the money to restore it. Also, the car had the steering wheel for the Ford Standard, rather than the fancier "Banjo" wheel for the Deluxe that was on American cars. Another unusual feature was the pair of side facing seats in the rumble seat area instead a single forward facing seat.

In May 1981, I communicated with a Denmark national, who was a member of the Early Ford V-8 Club. He provided me with the following information about Scandinavian-assembled Fords of the period:

> Scandinavian Ford used flathead V-8 engines with either the 21 studs per head (used in the US until 1937) or the 24 studs per head (correct for US manufactured Fords from 1938 onward) in the 1939 model year.
>
> The engine heads with the cast-in cylinder firing order were made in England. These engines were produced in the UK until 1954.
>
> The Deluxe model had the "Banjo" steering wheel, but not the leather upholstery.

I concluded that Scandinavian Ford used whatever engine configuration was on-hand during that pre-war timeframe. Since my car did not have the "Banjo" steering wheel, I assumed Ford used what they had on-hand.

My car came with cloth upholstery, and that jives with the data supplied from Denmark.

I communicated with Roland Swalas of Sweden, who owned a Danish 1935 Ford. His response is located in the Appendix. He clarified the unusual nameplate mounted on the engine firewall, as well as the location of the export data plate. The envelope was date stamped March 27, 1986. See the letter in the Appendix.

This 21 Stud Engine was delivered with my car. Note the cast-in cylinder firing order that was not on US made engines. I believe that this engine was made in England. Photo by Author

Roland provided this impression of his export data plate.

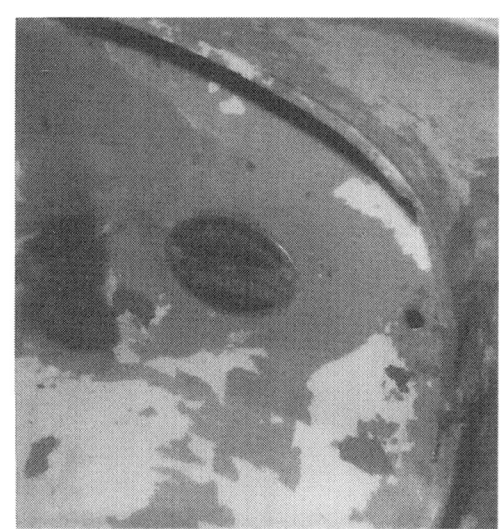

Photo provided by Roland Swalas of Sweden, depicting the firewall nameplate on his 1935 Danish Ford

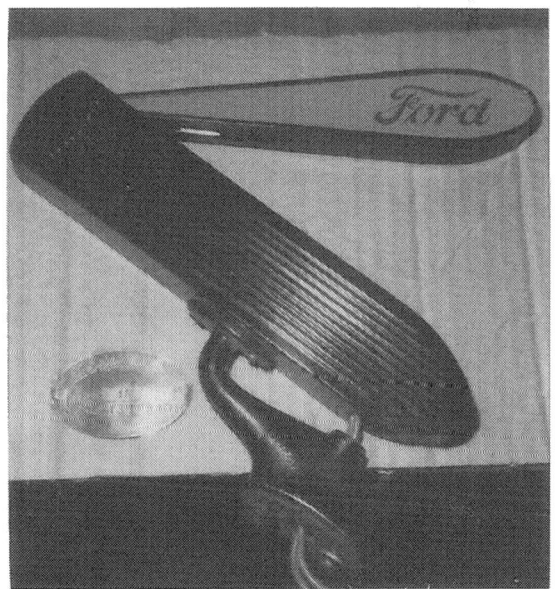

Photo of Trafficator, provided by Roland Swalas of Sweden, depicting the trafficator partially actuated. There is a light bulb inside the arm that illuminates the word, "Ford."

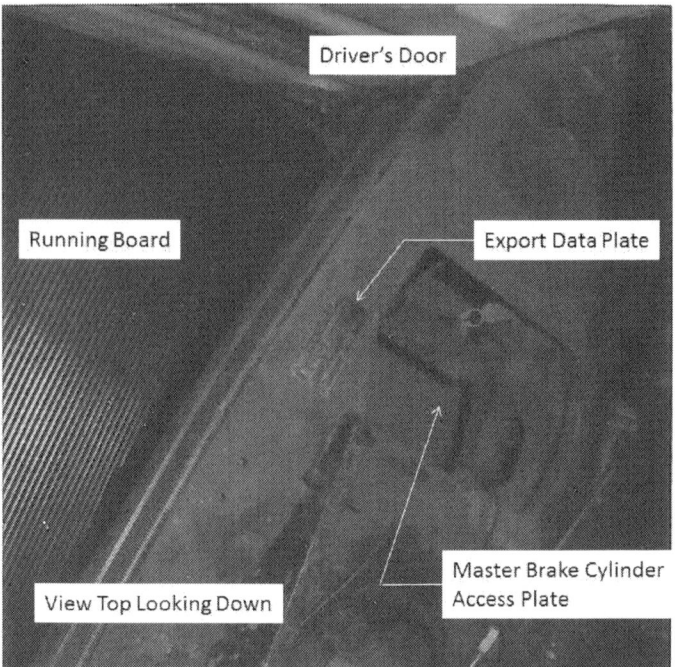

Driver's Door

Running Board

Export Data Plate

Master Brake Cylinder
Access Plate

View Top Looking Down

This photograph was provided by Roland Swalas of Sweden, depicting the location of the export data plate. The captions were provided by the author. Once the location of the plate was established, I made the decision not to reproduce it, as the car restoration costs were running out of sight, at the time, and the plate would be hidden by the rubber floor mat.

Roland's Danish 1935 Ford Roadster with trafficators

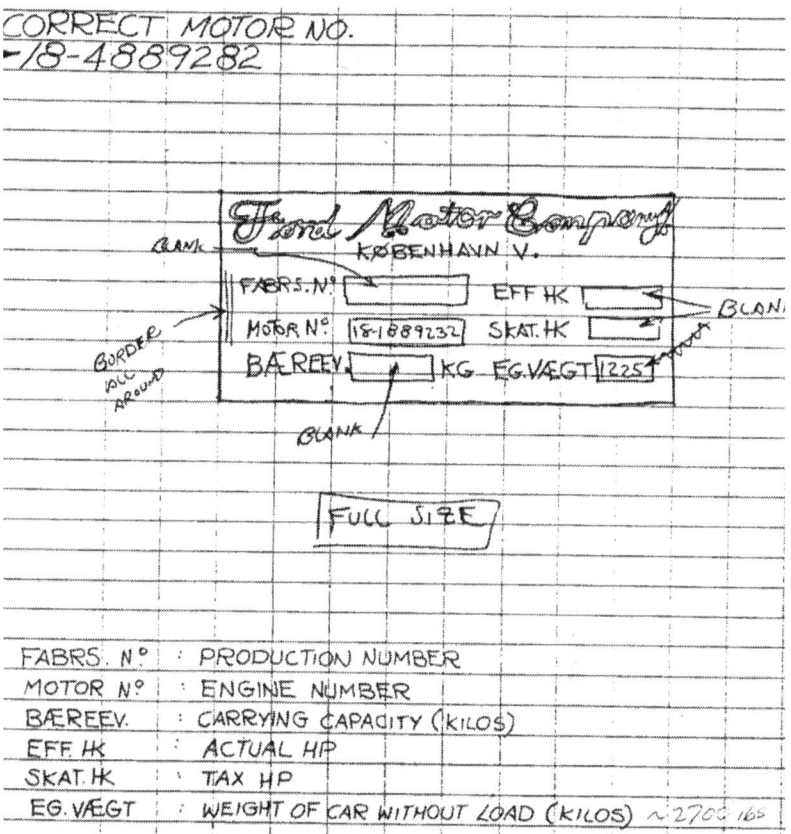

CORRECT MOTOR NO.
-18-4889282

| FABRS. N° | : | PRODUCTION NUMBER |
| MOTOR N° | : | ENGINE NUMBER |
| BÆREEV. | : | CARRYING CAPACITY (KILOS) |
| EFF HK | : | ACTUAL HP |
| SKAT HK | : | TAX HP |
| EG. VÆGT | : | WEIGHT OF CAR WITHOUT LOAD (KILOS) ~ 2700 lbs |

Sketch of Export Data Plate that came with my car

Trafficators: My car had European Trafficators mounted to the exterior of the firewall. However, the switch on the dash was missing. The photograph below depicts my restored car with the trafficators installed.

European Trafficators
Photo by Author

Trafficator actuated on my restored car
Photo by Author

The identification tag on the engine firewall was unlike American cars. I reused that foreign ID tag.

Unique Firewall Identification Data Plate on my Danish Ford
Photo by Author

THIS CAR IS CONSTRUCTED UNDER
UNITED STATES LETTERS-PATENT

OTHER PATENTS PENDING

Ford Motor Company

DETROIT, MICH. U.S.A.

Firewall Identification Data Plate on American Cars

In addition, the rumble seat cushion was unlike the American part. What was left of it indicated that the rumble seat was actually two seats facing each other.

Subsequent research revealed a wealth of information on the Danish Assembled Fords. The information that follows was obtained from an article in Old Cars Weekly, dated December 5, 1985,[27] concerning research on a Danish 1938 Ford coupe.

27

"..In the 1930s, foreign production of Ford cars was strictly by model number, not model year.

Lorin Sorenson, FoMoCo and Early V8 authority, explained it. He said overseas Ford assembly plants with surplus materials, or demand for certain models, simply continued production. The 1935 Model 48 Fordor sedan deluxe, for example, was assembled overseas from 1934 to 1939."

"Basically, the 1938 (the article addressed the 1938 model) Danish export models were identical to American Fords, but with slight modifications that enabled them to comply with that country's customs and safety standards.

For instance, my car (1938 Ford) had a metric speedometer, mechanical "trafficator" turn signals on the cowl sides, and combination red/amber taillights. Other than that, however, the Washington Blue coupe was 100 percent stock left-hand drive "American.""

This research explained the configuration of the engine not complying with that manufactured in 1939. The engine was of the configuration discontinued in America in 1937. It had 21 studs holding down each cast iron head, instead of the 24 studs used in 1938 through 1953, when the flathead engine was discontinued. The engine was one of those manufactured in England.

My car had the trafficators on the cowl. The speedometer was missing, so I was not able to confirm the metric readout. Also, one rear fender was missing, and the one I had didn't have a tail light.

1937 European Ford Woodie Spotted in Hawaii

Marilyn and I wintered in Hawaii after retirement, for 10 years. One day, we drove to the North Shore of Oahu, and spotted a 1937 Ford Woodie of European heritage. The car was right hand drive, and had the same trafficators that were on my 1939 Ford. One important difference; this car had the original switch on the dash that operated the trafficators. Up to this point, I had never seen the actual switch.

1937 Ford Woodie of European Manufacture        Left Hand Trafficator

Right Hand Drive

Note Trafficator switch

I spotted a 1937 Ford Woodie with Right Hand Drive, in Hawaii. Note the Trafficators and Switch on the Dash. The car was owned by the proprietor of an art store. He subsequently sold the car.

Close-up of European 1937 Ford Woodie
Note "Banjo" steering wheel and trafficator switch, in RH upper corner
Photos by Author

<u>I purchased my car and delivered it on October 27, 1979</u>
I made the purchase and arranged for pickup of the parts on a Friday, after my two sons took their Scholastic Aptitude Test (S.A.T.) exams for college entry. The seller offered the use of his contractor dump truck to haul the corroded parts to my home in Peabody, Massachusetts. As we were driving down the street that ran behind my house, I heard a neighbor say, "He'll never finish that." I was determined to prove him wrong. And I did.

10/27/79

DELIVERY OF PARTS
TO 39' FORD CONV CPE

Photos taken the day of delivery of the 1939 Ford Convertible Coupe Deluxe;
October 1979.  Photo by Author

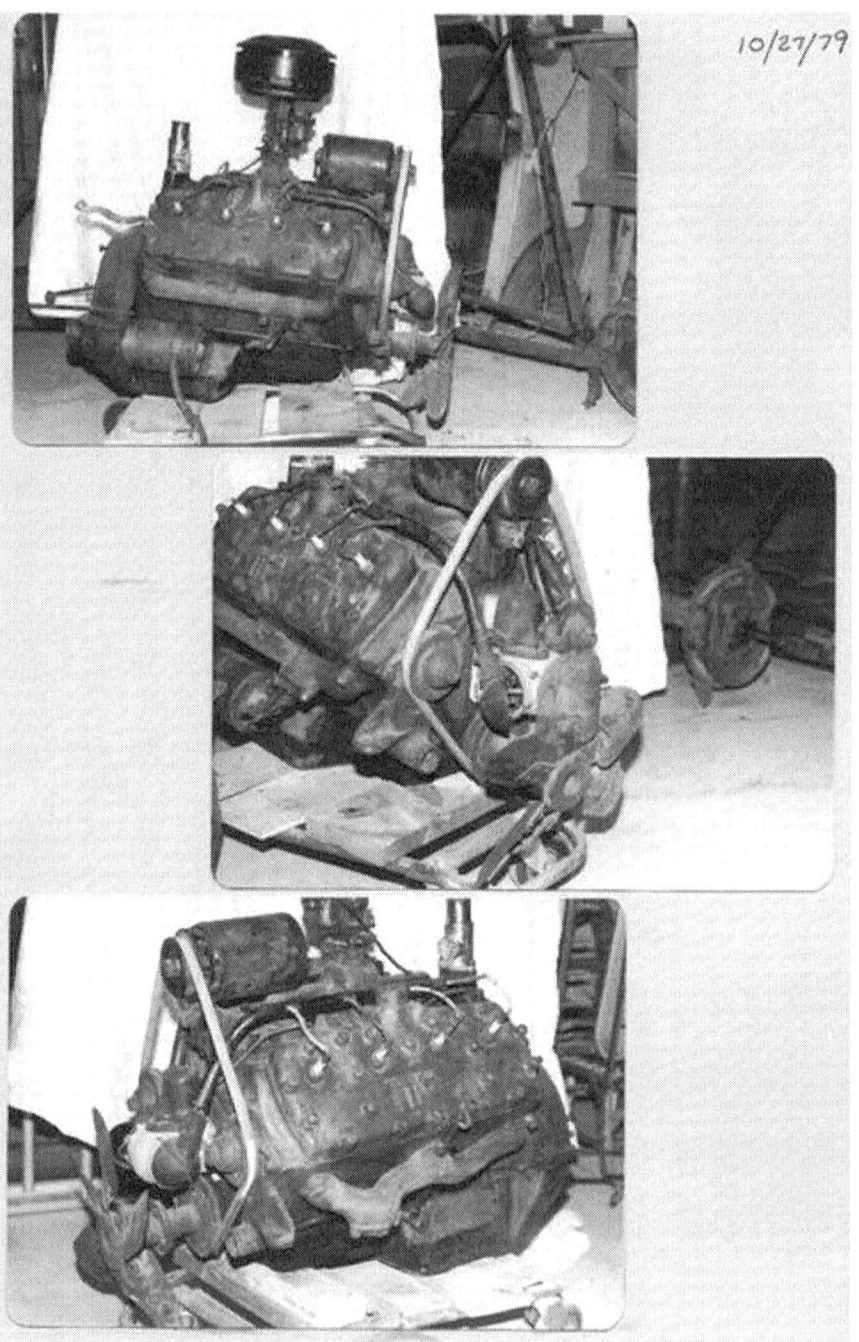

10/27/79

Photos taken of the engine for my 1939 Ford Convertible Coupe Deluxe; October 1979. Photo by Author

1939 Ford Cabriolet
A Ford Year in Transition

| *1939 Ford Models* | *1940 Ford Models* |
|---|---|
| Floor Shift ──────────→ | Column Shift |
| Rumble Seat ──────────→ | Gone |
| 4-Door Convertible ──────→ | Gone |
| Take Apart Head Lights ─────→ | Sealed Beam Headlights |
| Direct Reading Engine Temp Gage →  | Ignition Key Operated |
| Manual Convertible Top ──────→ | Vacuum Powered Top |

1939 Ford Offered for the first time
   Hot Water Heater (Previously Hot Air Heater)
   Hydraulic Brakes (Previously Mechanical Brakes)

# 1939 Ford Cabriolet

Assembled and Upholstered in Ford Copenhagen Plant
from Kit shipped from USA

Flathead V-8 Engine, 85 hp
Transmission 3 Speed, Floor Shift, 2nd/3rd Gear Synchromesh
6 Volt Electrical System, Positive Ground
Hot Water Heater
Rumble Seat
Rotomatic Radio
Directional Signal "Flippers" (European)

Dodge Brothers invented hydraulic brakes early in the 1930s, but it was rumored Henry Ford did not want to pay them royalties. Henry waited until the patent ran out, and then, in 1939, incorporated hydraulic brakes on his cars.

## Floor-Shift to Column-Shift Transmission

Floor Shift Transmission
Used in 1939 for the last time

Column Shift Transmission
Used in 1940

## Rumble Seat

The rumble seat was last used in 1939. Club Coupes were made prior to 1939 (back seat under the top instead of an exterior rumble seat). The Club Coupe was not made in 1939, but returned in 1940.

1939 Ford with Rumble Seat[28]

1940 Ford with back seat[29]

The engine hood was redesigned on the 1939 Ford Deluxe. On earlier Fords and on the 1939 Ford Standard, the engine hood was a shallow draw. The hood on the 1939 Ford Deluxe was a deep draw that facilitated maintenance on the engine without as much bending.

Radiator for 1939-1940 Ford

The radiator on both the 1939 and 1940 Fords was of the "split-core" design. In other words, there was a radiator for each of the left and right hand engine heads. In the middle, there was an access hole where a hand crank could be inserted, to hand crank the engine. When the Ford radiators were re-cored, typically the shop replaced the split-core with a single core design. I elected to go with the single core design because the cost was less.

In the 1939 Ford Deluxe, the engine cooling fan was relocated from the generator, and was bolted to the end of the exposed crankshaft.

---

29

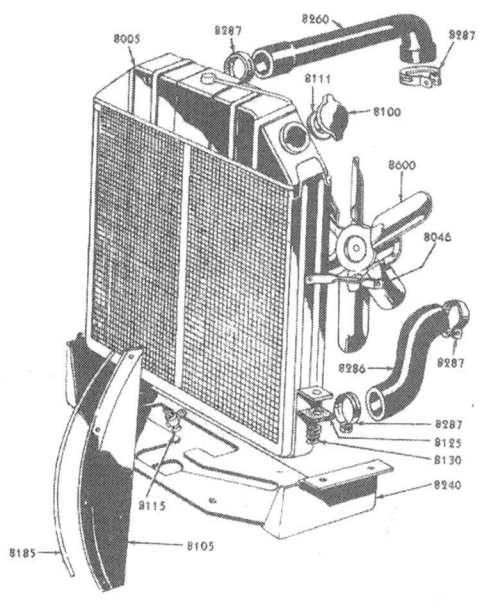

Split Core Radiator on 1939 and 1940 Fords[30]

## 1939 Ford Four Door Convertible

The four door convertible Ford was sold for the last time. It was discontinued in 1940. Photo by Author

---

The crank out windshield was last offered by Ford for the model year 1939, but not on convertibles and woody wagons.

Photo by Author

When the car was new, in 1939, the retail price for a 1939 Ford Convertible Coupe Deluxe in the United States was $745.

# FORD V-8 DELUXE

## Warranty

The Ford Motor Company warrants all such parts of new Ford automobiles, trucks and chassis, except tires, (see warranty below covering tires manufactured by Ford Motor Company) for a period of ninety (90) days from the date of original delivery to the purchaser of each new Ford vehicle or before such vehicle has been driven 4,000 miles, whichever event shall first occur, as shall, under normal use and service, appear to it to have been defective in workmanship or material. This warranty shall be limited to shipment, to the purchaser without charge, except for transportation, of the part or parts intended to replace those acknowledged by the Ford Motor Company to be defective. The Ford Motor Company cannot, however, and does not accept any responsibility in connection with any of its automobiles, trucks or chassis when they have been altered outside of its own factories or branch plants. If the purchaser shall use or allow to be used in the automobile, truck or chassis, parts not made or supplied by the Ford Motor Company, then this warranty shall become void. The Ford Motor Company does not undertake responsibility to any purchaser of its products for any undertaking, representation or warranty made by dealers selling its products, beyond those herein expressed.

The Ford Motor Company reserves the right to make changes in design and changes or improvements upon its product without imposing any obligation upon itself to install the same upon its products theretofore manufactured.

## Tire Warrranty

Every tire manufactured by the Ford Motor Company and bearing its name and serial number is warranted by it to be free from defects in workmanship and material, without limit as to time or mileage, and to give satisfactory service under normal operating conditions. If Ford Motor Company's examination shows that any tire has failed under the terms of this warranty, it will at its option either repair the tire or make an allowance on the purchase of a new tire.

The factory warranty was 90 days or 4000 miles, whichever came first.[31]

Chapter 8     The Restoration Starts

Locating a Restoration Shop and Securing Financing
After my two sons spent the morning taking their SATs for college entrance, we all went to pick up the parts. The seller had a dump truck, and he offered to help deliver the "car."

I spent the next six years pecking away at the restoration as I had a dollar or two available. I thought the hard part would be finding a source of financing. Suddenly, a new loan product became available, called a Home Equity Loan. I secured the necessary financing, and set about to locate a restorer. This, it turned out, became the hardest problem. I was turned down by two restorers as they were afraid of the immensity of the task.

Finally, I located an individual who was willing to take on the project as a challenge. He had the skills, as he was a precision sheet metal mechanic, by day, and an antique car restorer by night. He could do anything with sheet metal. We agreed on an hourly rate and the job began.

Parts Accumulation and Research on the Car Configuration
My friend from GE had a side business restoring antique car speedometers. After I purchased the 1939 Ford and before I started the restoration in earnest, I bought a new speedometer for my car from him. He had bought-out a defunct speedometer shop and part of the acquisition was a display case with a new and unused 1939 Ford Deluxe speedometer. It had been on display so long that the sun bleached a shadow behind the speedometer needle at Zero MPH. My friend calibrated the speedometer and sold it to me for $50.

Once the "car" was procured, it was necessary to gather all the manuals and books extant to thoroughly research the details of the 1939 Ford. Since the car was taken apart by the previous owner, I was at a disadvantage and had to learn how to assemble the restored parts. I attended all the local and not-so-local car shows in search of restored and original 1939 Ford Convertible Coupe Deluxe cars. When one was located, I tried to document as much as possible with my camera, and by talking to the owner. The appendix displays the various manuals that are currently available. The one published by the Early Ford V-8 Club was not in print when I was restoring my car. It has quite a bit of information that I could have used at the time.

1939 Ford Instrument Cluster[32]

1939 Ford Deluxe Speedometer

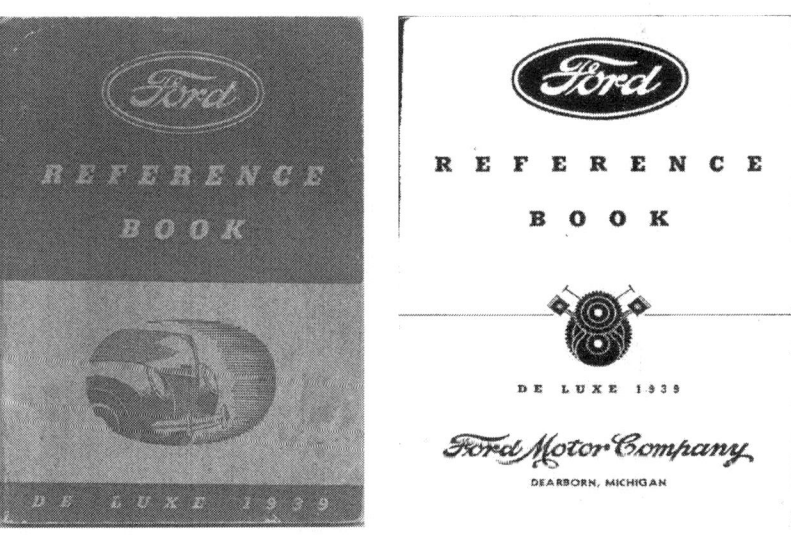

1939 Ford Owner's Manual[33]
This manual was a find, as it is not being reproduced

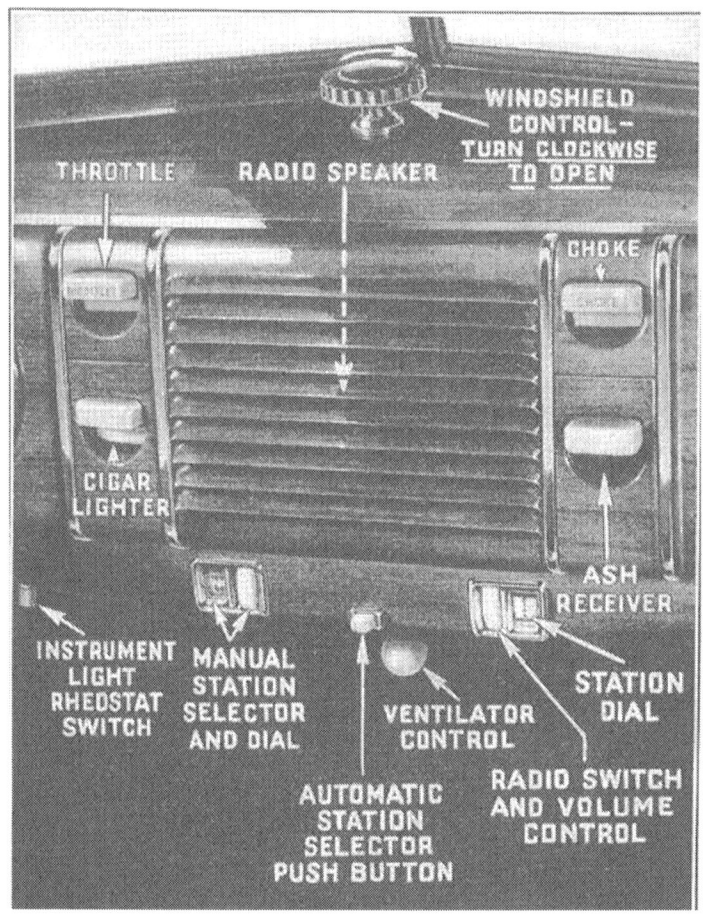

1939 Ford Deluxe Dash Controls

My convertible coupe deluxe was not equipped with a crank-out windshield. Accordingly, the upper "Windshield Control" knob was replaced with my windshield wiper knob, which was smaller.[34]

I purchased whatever sheet metal replacement parts that were available on the reproduction market. Of note was the trunk underdeck lid. Today, with shop labor rates upward of $100/hour, utilization of preformed sheet metal replacement parts is more economical than having them fabricated by hand.

---

34

1939 Ford Trunk Underdeck Lid

The trunk lid underdeck panel was available in reproduction form. The utilization of a preformed part such as this was more economical than repairing the original sheet metal. [35]

Once the collection of parts comprising my 1939 Ford was delivered, I took stock of the parts and their condition. A wire wheel attachment to my portable drill was used to grind away 47 years of accumulated dried mud and hardened oil residue. Difficult areas required the use of a scraper. I spent considerable time working on the frame, but in the end, I concluded it was too corroded and the body mounting riveted pads were not useable.

Now was the time to become an expert on the 1939 Ford Convertible Coupe Deluxe. After reading as much as I could find in the literature, I joined a local car club, The North Shore Old Car Club. Most car clubs put on a car show annually, with judging for the best cars. I volunteered to be on a judging team. I was not an expert, but I learned an immense amount of material. I made sure I was on the team that judged the class of cars that my 1939 Ford would be in, when finished.

---

[35]

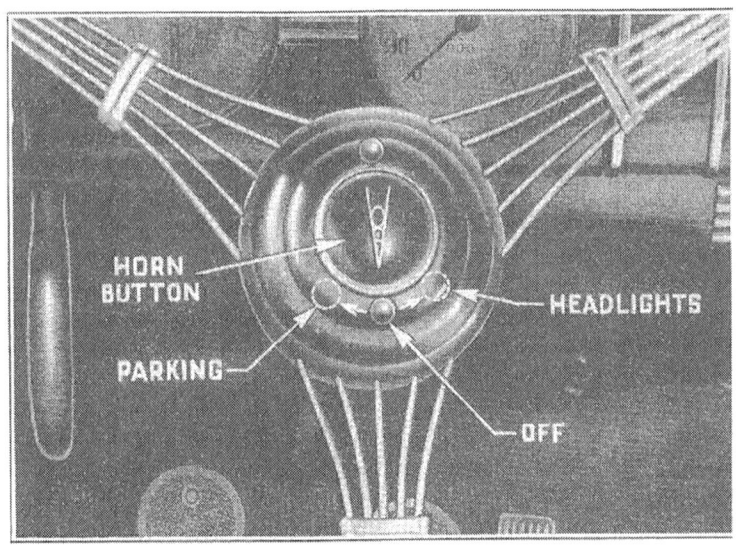

1939 Ford Deluxe "Banjo" steering wheel is depicted with the center horn and light switch.[36]

I made the decision to replace the frame. I located a 1938 Ford parts car in the local Want Advertiser. The frame from the 1938 Ford was the same as that for my 1939, even though the 1938 had accommodations for the mechanical brake system. The problem was the car was all together. I agreed to purchase the frame and steering assembly (the 1938 Ford had the "Banjo" steering wheel that was correct for 1938 and 1939 American cars), but the owner had to remove the body off the car. This was a monumental undertaking, and took a week of his concentrated effort.

My son, Scott, had inherited his grandfather's 1972 Ford Country Squire station wagon, which we used to deliver the frame and steering assembly. Actually, we drove directly to a Forge shop on the Lynnway, in Lynn Massachusetts, to have the frame sandblasted. Once this was accomplished, we supported the frame on four jack stands in one bay of my two-bay garage. I then painted the frame using multiple cans of red primer paint, then-top coated it with flat black paint.

---

Scott's 1972 Ford Country Squire Station Wagon used to transport frame to foundry for sand blasting of rust. The cost was $75. Photo by Author

I removed the cast iron heads from the delivered engine and observed a crack in the engine block, between a valve seat and a cylinder bore. This was not good. So, in addition to the engine being the wrong configuration for the American 1939 Ford model year, there was a crack. A repair procedure was available, but it was better to look for another engine block. I did not want to discover the repair was unsuccessful, later, when the engine was rebuilt and in the car.

The collection of rotted parts comprising my car did not come with either a radio or hot water heater, which were optional when the car was new. I located a heater from a 1940 Ford, which looked the same as the 1939 part. The heater control switch was a rare find. My son, Scott, located one for a 1941 Ford and installed it; the knob looked similar but was not exactly correct. Presently, the exact switch for the 1939 Ford is being reproduced, but I have no inclination to buy one.

There were a few small businesses that offered services repairing antique car radios. One year, I spent the entire paycheck from my two-week Air Force Reserve active duty tour, $450, to purchase a refurbished radio for the 1939 Ford. When installed, it sounded somewhat "tinny," but that was the quality of the car radio and speaker back then. I purchased a reproduction radio antenna and installed it in the car. Later, I assembled a "New Old Stock" spotlight. It required a 3/4 inch diameter hole be drilled in the windshield frame. I didn't want to remove the radio antenna, which ran within this windshield frame, so I gambled that the drill would miss the antenna lead. I gambled wrong. The drill bit bisected the antenna lead perfectly. A friend who repaired televisions for a living repaired the antenna lead. The lesson was, never take short cuts.

Drilled hole for spotlight and bisected radio antenna lead
Photo by Author

Rotomatic Radio for 1939 Ford.
Radio stations were preset using the knob on the left hand side.
Photo by Author
Note the "Wood Grain" paint.  It might have looked like a Jaguar, but it was, after all, a low priced Ford.

Overall view of the frame that came with the 1939 Ford
Photo by Author

## The Hunt for Parts

Attendance at flea markets was exciting because I never knew what I might find. The hunt was half the fun. In the 1970s and 1980s, old Ford flathead parts were plentiful at flea markets. Now, eBay has deflated the flea market culture. Sellers reach a bigger market instantaneously, and prices are higher.

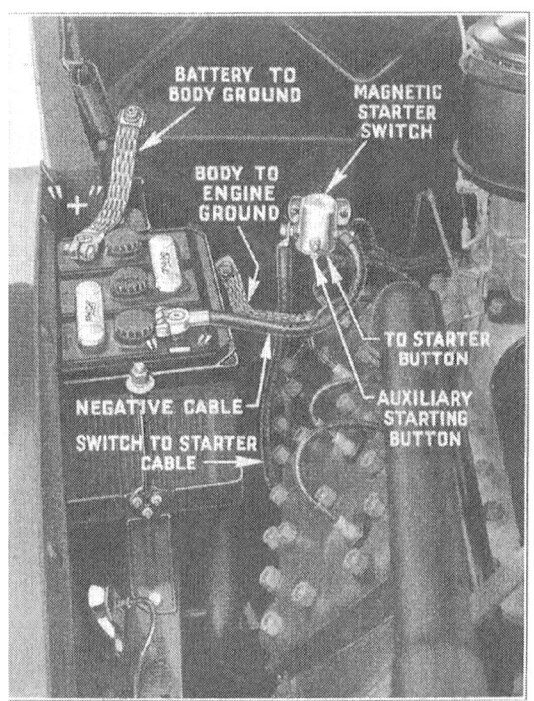

1939 Ford Deluxe Engine Compartment, Right Hand Side[37].
Note the battery positive ground strap, and the "Magnetic Starter Switch," otherwise called the starter solenoid. There is a button on the bottom of this component that acts as a starter button, to enable the engine to be started from the engine compartment.

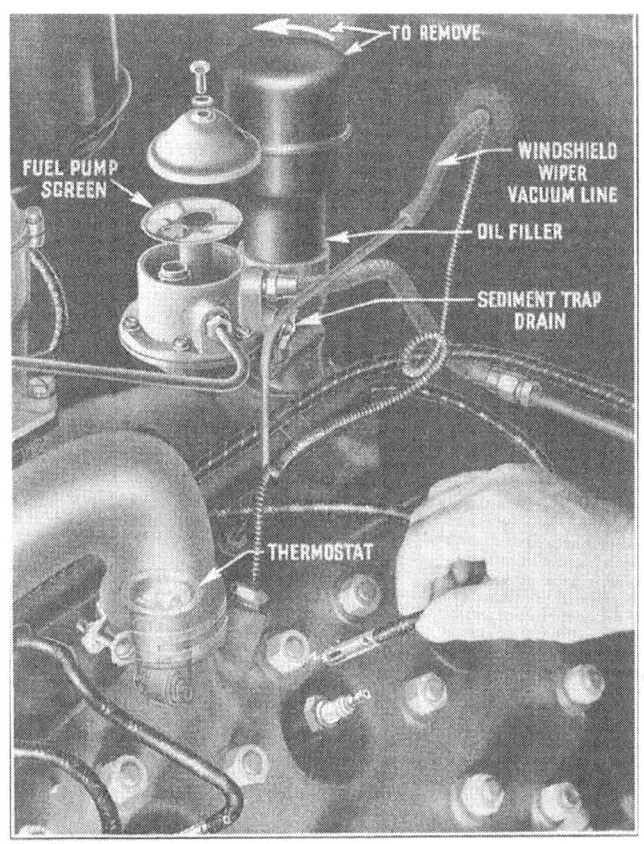

1939 Ford Deluxe Engine Compartment, Left Hand Side[38]
Note the part with the "pigtail" running from the firewall to the engine
block is the engine temperature gage sensor.

Many parts for old Fords were being reproduced. My experience
was many of these reproduction parts needed modification in order
to fit properly or to function. One part that comes to mind was the
headlight switch. I purchased a reproduction switch and it did not
work. Then I purchased a used original headlight wiring harness that
came with the switch attached. I used this harness and switch in my
restoration.

---

38

Mechanical parts were easy to find. There were many sources for new moving engine, transmission and rear end parts, such as pistons, main bearings, gears and so forth. There are still wrecking yards in rural parts of the country that have old cars piled up on top of one another.

Hemmings Motor News was an invaluable source for used and new parts, as well as suppliers of services and old cars for sale. This monthly magazine is still available at local news stands. I chipped away at restoring small parts early in the process; I worked on items that didn't cost much and were available in auto parts stores. This included the entire brake system. I was able to purchase all the hardware over the counter, as these parts fit a wide range of models. After five years, I had put aside a number of parts that were restored or refurbished, and painted. It was time for the serious restoration to begin.

The hard part proved to be convincing a restoration shop to undertake the project. One was recommended to me and the owner visited my garage on the way home from work. He said that he needed to locate a rust-free floor from a Ford in a western state. I never heard from him again. I think the required degree of restoration scared him.

I found an advertisement in Hemmings Motor News for a restoration shop. The proprietor had many years of experience in sheet metal fabrication and was a natural choice. He examined my rusted out hulk and agreed to undertake the work as a challenge. As indicated above, this was the shop I selected to restore my car.

The convertible top irons had pivot points that were worn. The proprietor had an acquaintance who was a retired machinist. He reversed engineered the parts for a reasonable sum. I purchased a pair of reproduction rear wheel skirts from a vendor advertising in Hemmings Motor News. The skirts were adequate but came with no integral mounting hardware. The restoration shop worked the magic with sheet metal, and modified them for use on my car. See Chapter 8 for details on the restoration of the body.

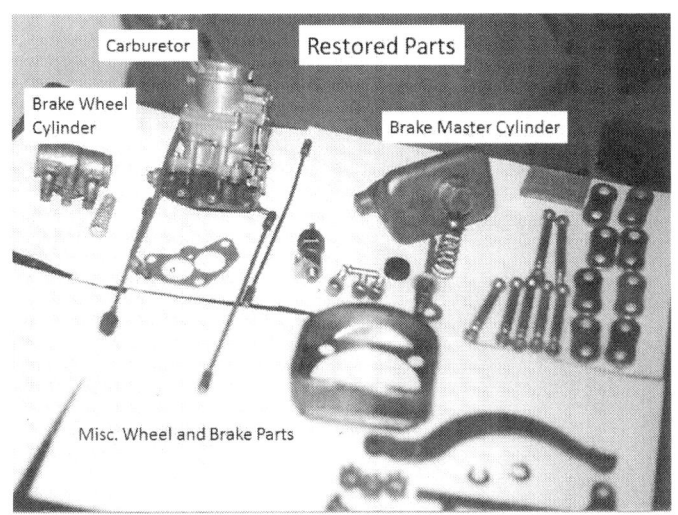

Restored parts waiting for the day they would be assembled in my car
Photo by Author

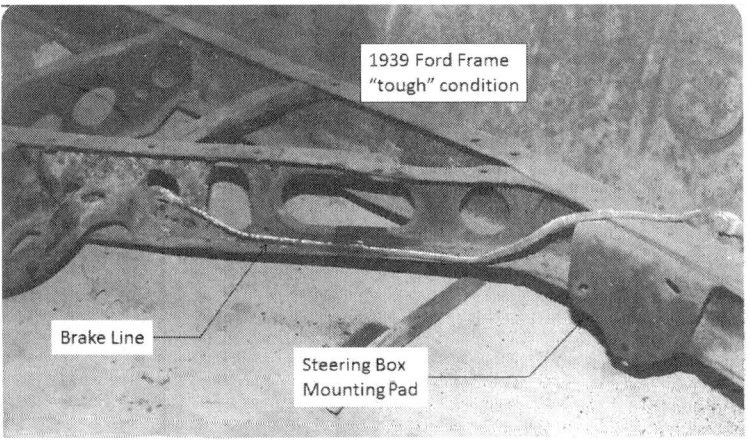

Close-up of the left-forward section of the 1939 Ford Frame. Note the corrosion in the frame on the left side of the photo
Photo by Author

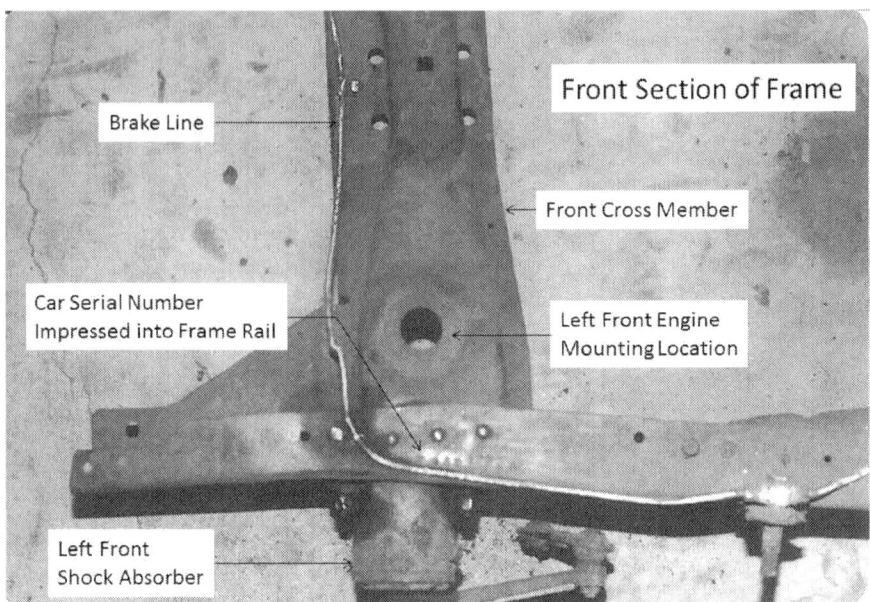

Brake Line

Front Section of Frame

Front Cross Member

Car Serial Number
Impressed into Frame Rail

Left Front Engine
Mounting Location

Left Front
Shock Absorber

The front section of the frame didn't look too bad. I used a wire wheel attachment to my portable drill to polish the area of the frame rail to expose the car serial numbers. Photo by Author.

I joined the Early Ford V-8 Club of America and the local New England Chapter. This was a wise move, as the national organization published an outstanding magazine six times a year. This periodical was full of technical tips and first hand experiences driving the old Ford. Membership also included a roster of all members, American and international. This was how I located members in Denmark and Sweden who provided me with the information on Danish manufactured Fords of the period.

I highly recommend the website, "earlyfordv8.org." This is a forum associated with the Early Ford V8 Club of America. People write – in requesting information about various subjects concerning the restoration or utilization of their old Fords, and "experts" respond. I learned something every time I visited that web site.

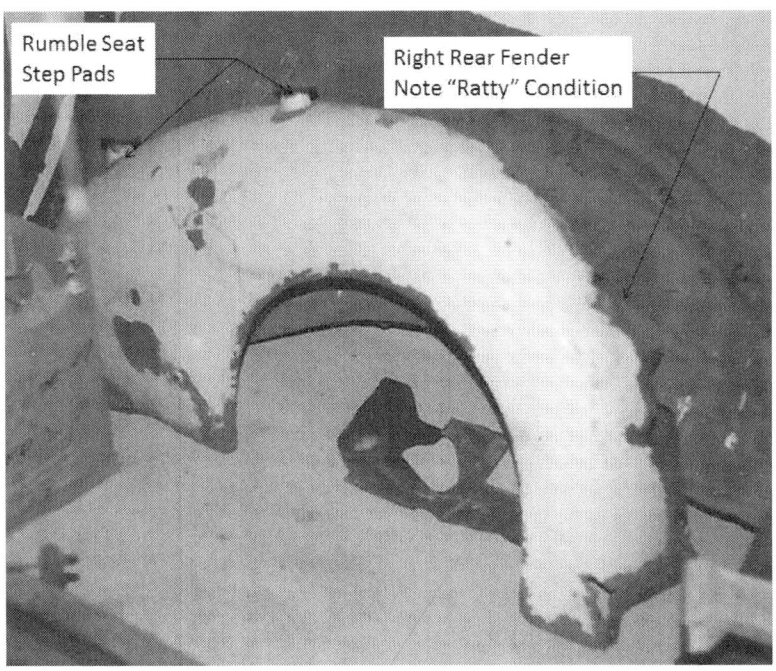

The car came with the front fenders, a spare front fender, and only one rear fender, the right rear. The rumble seat step pads were worth their weight in gold, as they were not being reproduced. Photo by Author.

I joined the North Shore Old Car Club (NSOCC) centered in Essex County, Massachusetts. Although this club was not car-make specific, the membership was over 300 car buffs, and many old Fords were represented. Also, there were a number of auto tradespeople in the club; these included an auto body shop owner, an auto glass shop proprietor, a retired auto mechanic and so forth. The contacts were well worth the annual membership dues.

A friend in the NSOCC purchased a 1939 Ford Tudor Deluxe, which he drove for a few years. After he sold the car, he contacted me and offered to sell a collection of pristine spare parts for the 1939 Ford Deluxe. I gladly paid the $200 asking price. This was quite a find.

Another friend came across a pair of headlight lenses for his 1939 Ford Standard Coupe. It turned out that the lens was slightly different between the Standard and the Deluxe. He gave me the lenses, as they fit my Deluxe. They were Ford "Script." This was what belonging to an old car club was all about; one member helping another.

Another friend had a box of WWII "A" gasoline ration stickers for the windshield. He sold me an original sticker for $1.00. It is mounted in the upper right hand corner of the passenger windshield glass.

I attended many cruise-in meets in my local area. These meets were held every week as long as the weather held up, from spring to fall. The purpose of the meets was manifold. First, it was a way to meet people in the hobby. Second, there was a chance to meet someone who had the same car that I was restoring, and who may have some spare parts that I needed. Third, many hobbyists were tradesmen; auto body or car mechanics, auto parts proprietors, etc. Many contacts were made at cruise-ins.

# 1939

## FORD PASSENGER CAR MODELS

**MODEL 91A FORD DELUXE**
*85 HP. 8-Cylinder Engine
(112" Wheelbase)

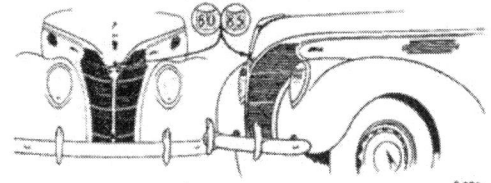

**MODEL 91A FORD STANDARD *85 HP. 8-Cylinder Engine**

**MODEL 922A FORD 60 HP. 8-Cylinder Engine**
(112" Wheelbase)

| BODY TYPE | NAME | BODY TYPE | NAME |
|---|---|---|---|
| 70-A | Standard Tudor Sedan | 76 | De Luxe Convertible Coupe |
| 70-B | De Luxe Tudor Sedan | 77-A | Standard (5-Window) Coupe |
| 73-A | Standard Fordor Sedan | 77-B | De Luxe (5-Window) Coupe |
| 73-B | De Luxe Fordor Sedan | 78 | Sedan Delivery |
| 74 | De Luxe Convertible Fordor Sedan | 79 | Station Wagon |

*Listed throughout Catalogue as 90 HP.

My car was a Model 91A; Body Type 76[39]
Note that the Deluxe (the upper view) is different from the Standard, below.  Also, note the "deep draw" engine hood on the upper "Deluxe" vs. the "shallow draw" on the "Standard," below.

---

39

---

I purchased this "Green Bible." This is an illustrated parts breakdown of all the chassis parts in antique Fords from 1928 through 1947.[40]

---

Chapter 9    Second 1950 Mercury Coupe

During the restoration of my 1939 Ford Convertible Coupe, a process that was going to take several years, I wanted an old car to drive around. I also wanted to join the NSOCC which was an active antique car club in the Essex County area. At the time, car ownership was a requirement to join.

The car of choice was a 1950 Mercury Coupe, the same car I owned as a teenager... I started searching and found an ad in the Boston Globe for a car that fit my needs. The seller was Boston Mercury. I could not find this dealer in the yellow pages under "Car Dealerships," but I called the telephone number anyway. Boston Mercury really was an individual named Jon, who puttered around, buying and selling cars and parts, especially 1949-1951 Mercurys. I arranged to meet him at a storage building in Boston to look at the car he had advertised. The building was crammed full of antique cars stored by various owners in the Boston area. One of several cars owned by Jon was a 1950 Mercury that had license plates welded together to form a floor in front of the front seat, where the original floor had rotted out. I passed on that one.

He had another 1950 Mercury for sale that met my needs. It was original, not restored, but was in remarkably good shape. It had dull chrome, some small rotted spots, but, overall, it was not in bad condition for a "driver." I noted that the rear window was the three piece assembly that was used in 1949; in 1950, Mercury converted to a one piece design. Jon had retrofitted the glass from one of his parts cars, for an unknown reason. I arranged to return the following week to give Jon time to move cars around in the storage building, and get the Mercury out and running. When I returned and tried to start the car, the starter did not crank. Jon told me that he put his "good" battery in the car, and that I was to hold pressure with my finger on the starter button for several seconds, and the starter would eventually crank. I did and it did! The test drive was satisfactory. Jon wanted $2,500 for the car, but took my offer of $2,250. The condition of my purchase was that he deliver the car to Peabody, where I lived, and I would give him a lift back to Boston.

My 2<sup>nd</sup> 1950 Mercury Coupe.
I subsequently replaced the mismatched tires with a full set of new bias ply wide whitewalls.  Note the three piece rear window that was correct for the 1949 model.
Photo by Author

I am following in love all over again
Photo by Author

This was a "driver," but a nice "driver." I wish I still had this car.
Photo by Author

There was an interesting coincidence; Jon also owned a 1939 Ford Convertible Coupe, the same model car I was restoring. His car was a survivor, not restored, and was purely a driver. When I told him I had bought the same car, he said that he had looked at the car I bought, and passed. He didn't feel it was a good purchase, even as a parts car.

I set out to make the Mercury more to my needs. I had a custom dual-exhaust system installed, with glass-pack mufflers. Boy did that engine sound nice! Next, I purchased a set of wide whitewall tires. The car radio didn't work, so I contacted an antique car radio repair shop in Marblehead, Massachusetts. The owner told me about a design defect in the 1950 radio model, and would not recommend I repair my radio, but that he had a restored 1951 Mercury radio for sale. The 1951 model looked the same externally. I paid $150 for the radio and put it in myself.

The directional signal lights did not work. Inspection revealed that the wires were not hooked up to the switch under the steering wheel. I had a wiring diagram for the car, and knew from the color coding which wire went where, but the color coding on the original wires had faded, and I was not able to discern which color was which. I didn't hook up the directional lights.

## My Ignition Coil Failed

I had attended a NSOCC meet at a member's house in Newberry, Massachusetts, one Sunday. It was a combination picnic and old parts auction. I purchased a New Old Stock (NOS) spotlight for my Ford. I had just started to drive home and, perhaps two miles down the road, the engine quit. Another club member came by and we tried to get the car running, unsuccessfully. It was obviously an ignition problem. My friend went home, hooked up his car trailer to his SUV, returned and towed me home. Subsequent troubleshooting revealed that the ignition coil had failed. I was able to buy a new one at an auto parts store and install it myself. While I was at it, I replaced all the ignition wires, spark plugs, distributer cap, rotor, points and condenser. I was not going to break down again!

## My Car was a Movie Star

The local public television station contacted me and requested my car be used in a movie that was to be shot in Summerville, Massachusetts. I believe the name of the movie was "The Education of Emily." In the movie, a man traded-in his older Buick at a small used car lot, for a later model Hudson. The deal turned sour when the Hudson broke down, as it was a "lemon." Emily told her husband to return the car, but her husband refused because he knew there was no way a used car dealer would take back a car. Emily wouldn't take "No" for an answer, and convinced the dealer to reverse the trade.

The movie was shot at a 1950s-looking used car lot. My Mercury was put on the lot in the front row as a prop. I had to be there for 12 hours while the scenes were shot. During that time, unsavory characters walked by the shoot.

I was paid "scale" which was $50 for my trouble. I used the money to buy a new six-volt battery for the car. The movie writer was a former used car dealer. He disparagingly referred to my car as a "Junker." I didn't appreciate his comments, but I felt he was low class and not worthy of arguing with.

## My Merc and the Beach Boys

I drove the Merc to work one nice summer day to show it off to my co-workers. At lunchtime, I left the plant to get gas. As I departed the gas station, I tuned in the local 50s radio station; it was playing a "Beach Boys" song. I got so pumped up that I attempted to accelerate hard in first gear, drop the clutch and speed shift into second. As I did this, the shift lever suddenly went limp in my hands. I was disconnected from the transmission. Oh, Oh! I coasted to a stop on the side of the road. Across the street was Lynn Hospital. A gentleman in the parking lot saw me disabled and walked over. He was an old car buff. He put the transmission in second gear by moving the shift levers at the transmission, under the hood, and I nursed the car home in second gear about 10 miles. I located a replacement steering column with a good shift tube and replaced the unit on my car. Examination of the part that came off the car revealed that the shift tube within the steering column had a "dog" that was spot welded on and it had sheared off.

## Transmission Lockup

Marilyn and I had attended a club event, and were returning home in the Merc. I was within one half mile of the house, had turned off the main road and shifted from third back to second gear. I must have rushed the shift because the transmission couldn't make up its mind which gear to go into, and split the difference. Basically, it locked up. A passerby, who was a mechanic, stopped and offered assistance. I jacked up the car by the rear end and we rocked the car back and forth until the transmission gears sought a neutral position. Unfortunately, the car fell off the jack, pried open the differential cover plate, and leaked the differential fluid out. I slowly drove the car the rest of the way home without fluid. I bought/installed a used cover from an ad in Hemmings Motor News, and serviced the oil, but was never able to completely seal this unit. I always had a small seepage.

## I Sold the Merc

As my 1939 Ford was nearing completion, I sold the 1950 Mercury for $3,500. I broke even considering the initial cost of $2,250 and the cost of the improvements I made. The new owner painted the car gloss black, without fixing the corrosion, but it looked presentable. He also figured out how to wire the directional signals, so I have to give him credit. I saw the new owner and the Merc a couple of times, and I understand that he sold the car to someone on Cape Cod. I never saw the car again.

## I Thought the Mercury was out of my System

In Amesbury, there was a company named LeBarron Bonney that specialized in fabricating kits to upholster antique Fords. They took in a selected few cars to upholster on-site, but there was a waiting list. I was selected. When I brought the 1939 Ford to LeBarron Bonney, to have the upholstery and convertible top installed, there was a 1951 Mercury Convertible in the shop at the same time, having upholstery work done. I fell in love with the Mercurys of that era all over again! What I wouldn't do to have the car today. They are out there, but the asking prices are in the mid-teens.

As described earlier, the engine that came with the car had a crack in the cast iron block. In 1980, I located a 1941 Ford parts-car on a used car lot in Lynn, Massachusetts. The engine had the outward appearance of the 1939 engine that was desired for the restoration. I purchased the parts-car for $395 and had it towed to my house. While the car was in my driveway, I stripped out the seats and any other soft parts that could be hiding vermin, and disposed of them. Then I pushed the car into my garage and started disassembly and cleaning of the parts in earnest. My objective was to store any parts I would need for my restoration, and sell off the remainder to recover my investment.

After removing the engine from the car, and storing it in my basement, I disassembled the rest of the car, sold off parts to hobbyists restoring a 1941 Ford, and junked the remaining carcass. My investment was made back, and I had the engine for free. Next, I removed the engine heads and discovered the engine was seized up, probably from rust. This was surmountable, so the engine was put aside in my basement to be rebuilt later.

I placed an ad in my company newspaper to sell parts from the car. The owner of a florist shop in Swampscott responded immediately. He forgot to set the hand brake on his antique 1941 Ford coupe, and the car rolled back into a telephone pole. I sold him quite a few parts. I was well on my way toward making back my initial investment.

1941 Ford Convertible[41]

41

I pushed my 1941 Ford Tudor parts-car into one bay of my two car garage.
Photo by Author

My 1941 Ford parts car with the front end removed. The car looks a little "bent."
Note the hood leaning against the wall, on the right. I sold the hood for $25 to a
man who acted as if I was stealing food from his baby!
Photo by Author

Close-up of the engine compartment, with the front end sheet metal removed
Photo by Author

Another close-up view of the engine compartment, with the front end sheet metal removed. Photo by Author

This is a top view looking down at the engine compartment. Note the rotted battery box on the left, carburetor in the center rear, generator in center front, accessory bypass oil filter on the right, and twin horns on the far right. Photo by Author.

I met a variety of characters while selling the parts. One man was downright nasty. He acted as if I was stealing food from the mouth of his child. Another negotiated using hardball tactics, a ploy that I did not appreciate.

Still another drove all the way from Southern Connecticut. He had a nephew who was trying to straighten out from a tough childhood. This man was helping the youngster restore a 1941 Ford as a joint project. He bought most of my remaining parts, and I broke even dollar-wise at this point. And, I had the engine for free. Unfortunately, parts cars are now scarce, as the word got around how lucrative used parts could be.

I sold the transmission for $75, and thought I made a killing. In 1940, Ford changed from a floor-shift to a column-shift transmission, so I felt justified in selling the assembly. Later, when I got around to restoring the transmission for my 1939, I removed the top shifter cover plate, and was shocked to discover that there was about an inch of rust-colored water in the bottom of the casing, and no oil. The internal parts, gears, spacers, synchronizers, and bearings were corroded beyond recovery. Research indicated that both the floor-shift and the column-shift units utilized the same "guts;" gears, bearings, synchronizers, and spacers. I screwed myself by selling the transmission from the 1941 Ford. I bought a floor-shift transmission from a 1936 Ford at an antique car flea market for $65. As a floor shift unit, it interchanged with the 1939, and I did not have to rebuild it, as it looked good upon inspection.

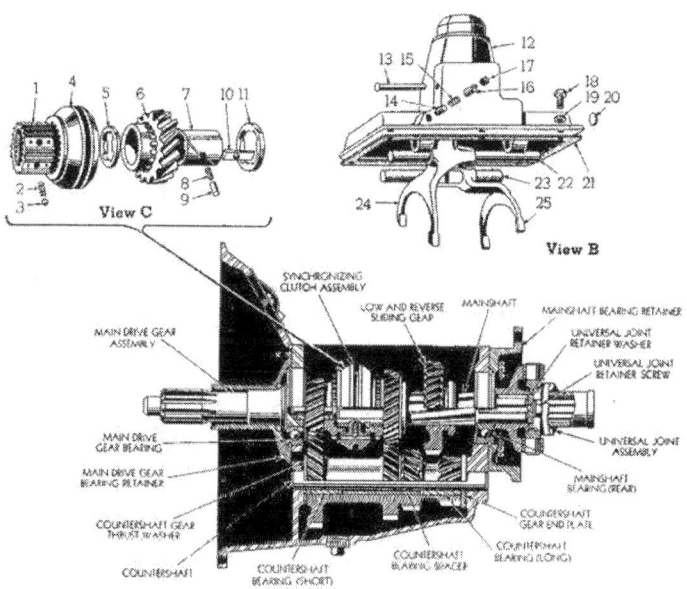

All these floor-shift transmission internal parts are interchangeable with the column-shift unit on the 1941 Ford.

Ford Top Shifter Transmission[42]

---

42

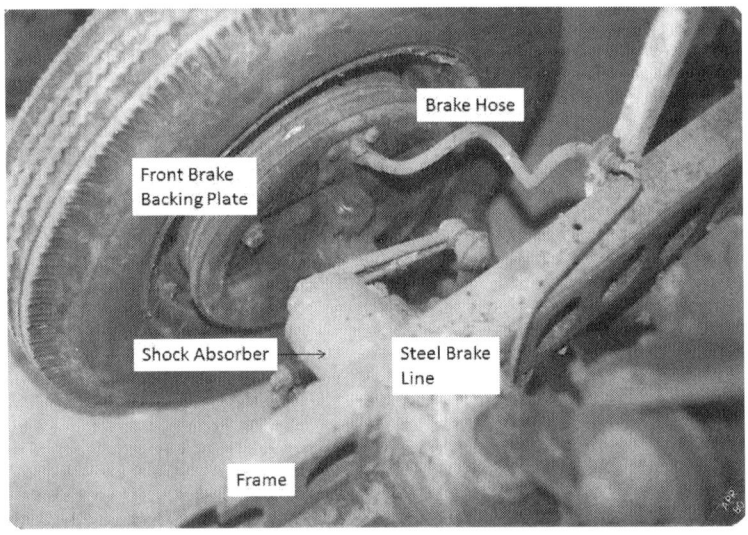

Right front wheel assembly.
Note the unusual Houdaille shock absorber assembly
Photo by Author

There were many parts that were common with my 1939 Ford, such as much of the brake system, shock absorbers, and lots of fasteners. I saved everything.

Quite a bit later, I had the restored chassis for the 1939 Ford in my garage. This consisted of a rolling frame, complete brake system, complete drive train and suspension, all prettied up with a fresh coat of paint in original colors. The "bad" frame was at the restoration shop and was used as a fixture to build up the body as it was being restored. It was time to bring the restored chassis to the shop, in order to mount the restored body onto the chassis. I came across a hot rod shop that needed a frame for a project. The owner proposed I swap the frame from the 1941 Ford for a tow of the chassis to the shop. It was a win-win. But, I have gotten ahead of the story.

There were many parts that were junk, such as the fenders and dashboard. I simply put these parts out for collection by the local trash man. All that was left of the 1941 Ford was the bare sheet metal body, which was worthless to me. I called a local junkyard and they picked up the remaining body gratis.

Chapter 11    Rebuilding the Engine on the 1939 Ford

The day finally arrived. It was time to delve into rebuilding the engine. The unit that came with the disassembled car was actually correct for the 1937 Ford (USA manufactured engine), but had that crack I described earlier. While there was a welding procedure to repair this crack, it was not an optimum solution, and there could be problems later on with the repair. I made the decision to look for another engine to rebuild, based on both the obvious discrepancy in appearance and the crack. My plan was to use the engine from the 1941 Ford parts car.

21 studs held down each "Head"
on 1937 Ford Engine
(24 studs used on my 1939 Ford )

1937 style engine came with my disassembled 1939 Ford
Photo by Author

However, while scanning the local "Want Advertiser," in the antique car section, I found an ad for a 1940 Ford engine. The owner lived in South Peabody, so I made an appointment to see the engine. He obviously didn't have both oars in the water. He had owned a 1940 Ford, years ago, and replaced a slipping clutch, but it continued to slip after the repair. He tore down the car to save the engine, transmission and rear end, stored the assemblies in his back yard under a tarpaulin, and junked the rest. It was now many years later, mice had made a home in the engine, and it was seized up from rust. I made an offer of $50 for the engine, but the owner didn't react. The next day, I called and offered $100 for the whole drive train; engine, transmission and rear end. The deal was made. My son, Scott, had inherited his grandfather's 1972 Ford station wagon, so we used it to transport the heavy parts home. (The cast iron engine, alone, weighed about 500 pounds.)

Now there were three engines, and a decision had to be made as to which one to rebuild. I partially tore down the engine from the 1940 Ford to discover that the engine was actually a 1939 model. This was confirmed by the serial number that was exposed when the cast iron heads were removed. Also, the engine did not have a rear seal as specified on the 1940 models; it had a windback, or "slinger," which was correct for 1939. I made the decision to rebuild this engine. I stripped it of removable parts and brought it to an engine machine shop near the GE, where I worked. Engine machining was a highly specialized task, requiring expertise and expensive tooling, so I wasn't about to tackle this work by myself. The machining work cost somewhere in the $850 range, which would be a bargain today.

My research proved the engine was actually from a 1939 Ford, as indicated below:

> Engines made in 1942 had serial numbers starting with 18-6769036
>
> Engines made in 1941 had serial numbers starting with 18-5896295

Engines made in 1940 had serial numbers starting with 18-5210701

**The engine I used had serial number 18-4843967, confirming the 1939 engine.**

Engines made in 1939 had serial numbers starting with 18-4661001

Engines made in 1938 had serial numbers starting with 18-4186447

The block was rusted shut. The machinist used a sledge hammer and chisels to break the pistons out of the seized up cylinders. The sledge hammer was used to free up the valves so that they could be removed. After the machining work was completed, I paid the bill and brought the block home. I planned to assemble the new pistons, valves, etc. myself. The engine block was mounted to my engine stand and assembly of the pistons was about to begin, when I saw what looked like a fine crack in one of the machined cylinders.

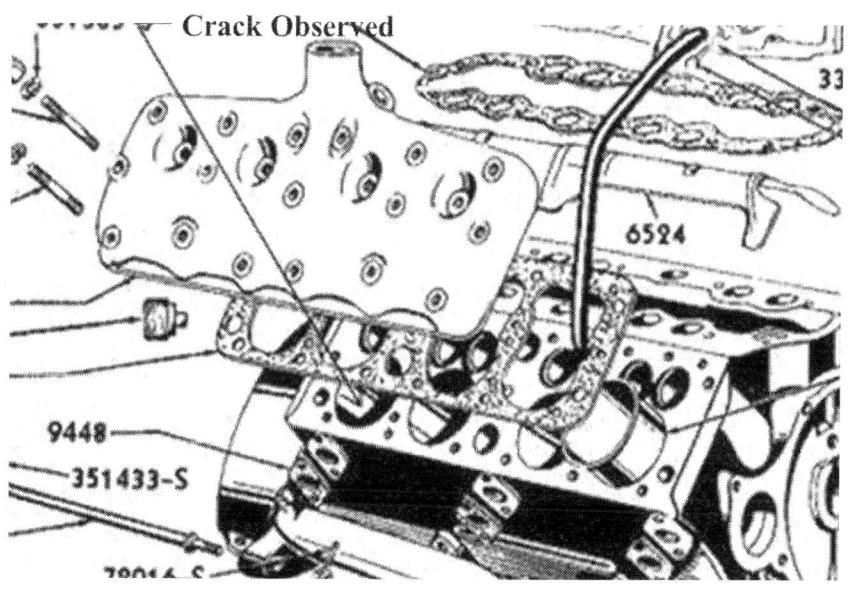

My engine had a airline crack in a cylinder bore[43]

43

I returned the engine block to the machine shop, and they confirmed my diagnosis. I was disappointed that they didn't discover the problem when they were working on the block, but the only solution was to bore the cylinder oversize, insert a "sleeve" in the cylinder with the crack, and machine the sleeve to the same diameter as the other "unsleeved" cylinders. I then assembled the engine and painted the exterior with the correct Ford-green paint.

Engine Oil:    After I restored my Ford, I decided to utilize the same engine oil that was available in 1939; SAE 30 non-detergent oil. This oil was all that was available back then. The tendency of the flathead Ford engine to run hot led to a frequent breakdown of the oil (over-temperature of the oil leading to the formation of sludge). After a few years, I changed over to modern SAE 10W-30 engine oil that had many additives beneficial to the engine life. The procedure was to drain the SAE 30 oil, fill the crankcase with kerosene and run the engine for a few minutes, to dislodge any sludge and carry it in suspension. Next, the kerosene was drained and the SAE 10W-30 was added. To my knowledge, since the restoration, my engine has never had a buildup of sludge. I religiously changed the engine oil at the end of each driving season in preparation for storage in my garage, for the winter.

The 1939 Ford was offered with an optional oil filter. My car was not equipped with one, but the 1941 Ford parts car that I purchased (See Chapter 10), did have the accessory. I utilized the latter filter. These oil filters were nowhere near as efficient as those used today. This accessory was a bypass design. In other words, the engine oil pump diverted a portion of the pressurized oil through the filter. Today's filters are in line with the full discharge of the oil pump, and do a more efficient filtration of the engine oil.

The 1941 Ford parts car came with the accessory bypass oil filter, which I incorporated into my restoration. Photo by Author

The Ford flathead engine required periodic grinding of the engine valves. This process used grinding compound to precisely match the valve sealing surface with the engine valve seat. Backyard mechanics were capable of performing this grind process. Typically, old Fords required this operation at about 40,000 miles. Also, the engine needed to have the piston rings replaced. I attribute these maintenance actions to the oil technology available in the day. By 100,000 miles, if the car made it to this point, it was shot and needed replacement.

## Restoration Advice

### Spare mechanical parts

This is as good a point as any to cover the subject of spare parts. Mechanical parts for old Fords are readily available, both as newly manufactured and as NOS (New Old Stock). Consult Hemmings Motor News for a list of sources for pistons, bearings, gears, etc. Also, the same reference is best used for rebuild services for many parts and assemblies. Anybody and everybody doing work on old cars advertises in Hemmings Motor News.

I highly recommend joining the Early Ford V-8 Club of America and the nearest local chapter. There is a wealth of technical information available just for the asking. Also, you will meet members who will be willing to lend you a hand in performing mechanical work on your car, if you are so inclined.

Also, if a local antique car club is found, join it. I joined the clubs referenced above as well as the local NSOCC. This latter club is not marque specific, but the contacts and comrade were terrific, and I had a lot of fun driving to meets and tours.

Many old Ford parts are being produced, new. You can purchase new carburetors, fuel pumps, gas tanks, fenders, water pumps etc. However, be prepared for surprises. Just because a part is new doesn't mean that there will not be failures. I refer to these failures as "infant mortality." It has happened to me regularly.

Surprisingly, NAPA Auto Parts can sometimes order a part for an old Ford. If it is stocked, it can be shipped to the retailer overnight.

Chapter 12    Restoration of the Body

I obtained catalogues from all the antique Ford parts suppliers and purchased just about everything available. I scanned Hemmings Motor News monthly for advertisements of parts for sale from fellow hobbyists and from parts-cars. This was the way I found such items as a hot water heater, new front and rear leaf springs, a refurbished radio (from an antique car radio restoration source) and so forth. The UPS delivery man for my area knew my house. He just raised the garage door and put the package inside without trying to track me down, if I was not home.

The search was on for old Ford parts at many antique car flea markets within a reasonable radius of my home. I usually came home with something, even if the part was already available. I never knew what would be needed going forward. I came home with spare fuel pumps, carburetors, distributors, coils, and so forth. Most of these parts were not used in my restoration, but I felt I was making progress by simply buying the spare parts.

There were several tire companies reproducing the tire styles and construction (bias-ply tires) of the period, wide whitewall and all. Ford sold tires under their name in those days, and reproduction Ford tires were available. I elected to purchase the Firestone reproduction tires with whitewalls. Also, the correct wide whitewall tire had whitewalls on both the outside and inside of the tire. These were called double whitewalls, but I elected not to spend the extra money.

Bias ply tires had a natural tendency to follow every dip and pothole in the road. That is why the driver of the day constantly adjusted the steering while driving. There is a saying, "Bias ply tires pick up bumps that radial tires forgot about." This can be observed in movies of the period. The camera was set up on the engine hood looking at the driver, and he/she was constantly adjusting the steering to stay in the driving lane.

My car was equipped with reproduction Firestone bias-ply wide whitewall tires with tubes. Radial tires are now available for the old cars, wide whitewalls and all. These radials make a world of difference in how the car drives. However, the cost per tire is high.

I must admit that my restoration was particularly hard, because I did not take apart the car. If I had, I could have documented the disassembly with photographs that would have helped on the reassembly. I just had an incomplete collection of distressed parts. In my research, I discovered a diagram of the assembled body of the car with key dimensions. This find was invaluable in the reassembly. (See illustration on the opposite page.)

The first step in the restoration was to deliver the parts to a chemical stripper, to remove all the paint and traces of rust.[44]

The following is an abbreviated discussion on the sheet metal restoration. A shop may be able to provide an estimate of the restoration cost, but it may not be too accurate. The problem is, once the car is disassembled, more and more corrosion damage may be revealed that was not in the estimate. This was not the fault of the shop. It was just the way it was. My recommendation is to take any estimate and double it. As the job progresses, be prepared to have an open checkbook. For this reason, I recommend buying the car already restored.

---

44

## 1939 Deluxe Convertible Coupe 91A-76
### NUMBER PRODUCED: 10,422

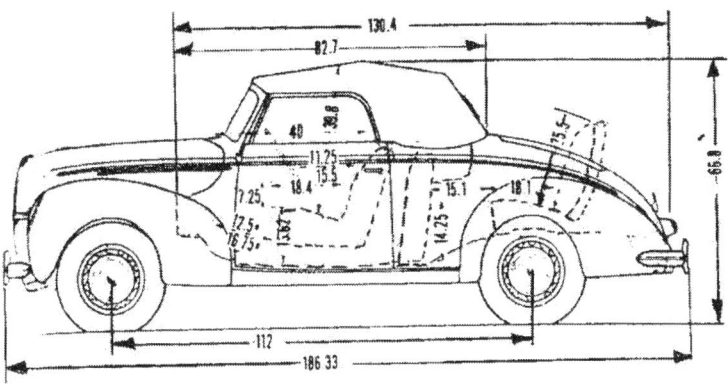

1939 Ford Deluxe Body Dimensions[45]

One of the areas that needed complete restoration on my car was the lower door sections, up to about six inches from the bottom. The sheet metal was completely gone. That was nothing compared to the floor. It was completely detached from the body, and needed full restoration. Luckily, the left and right floor sections were being reproduced with all the correct stiffening ribs.

However, the tunnel tying the floor sections together needed to be constructed from scratch, and welded into the left and right sections. The remnants of the original tunnel were used to reverse engineer a new one and the left and right floor pans were welded to this tunnel. I noticed, recently, that the entire floor is now available, including the tunnel welded to the LH and RH floor sections.

45

Lower six inches were reproduced
By the restoration shop and welded in

The bottom six inches or so were fabricated by the restoration shop and welded in.  It was impossible to tell where the new section began and ended.[46]

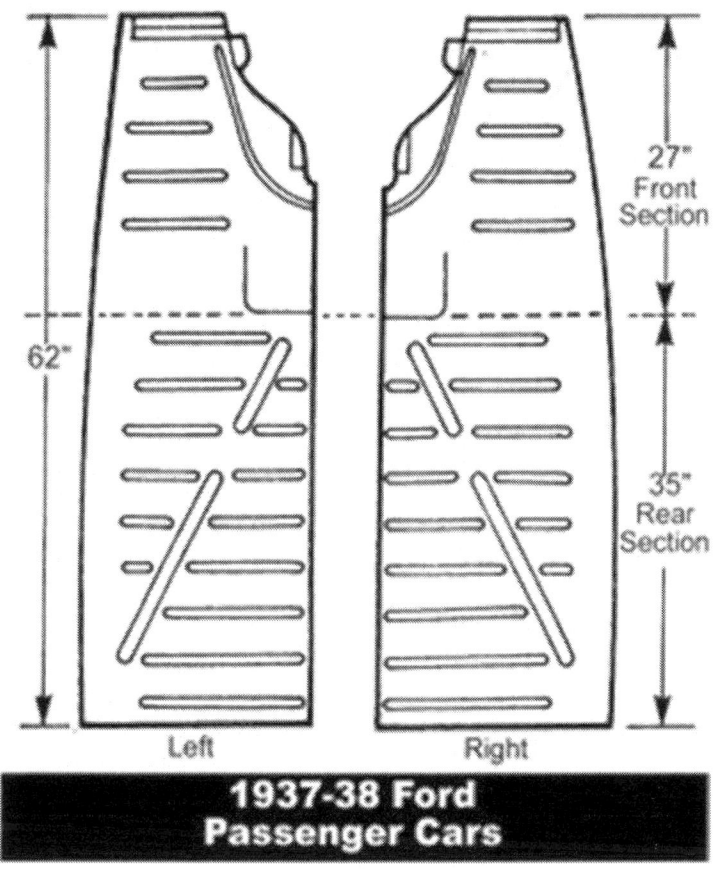

Reproduction floor pans purchased from Bradley Floor Pans[47]

The sheet metal restoration and painting of the car were processes that required expertise and were labor intensive. These tasks took considerable time. The photographs that follow give the reader a glimpse of the work involved, without bogging down with detail.

47

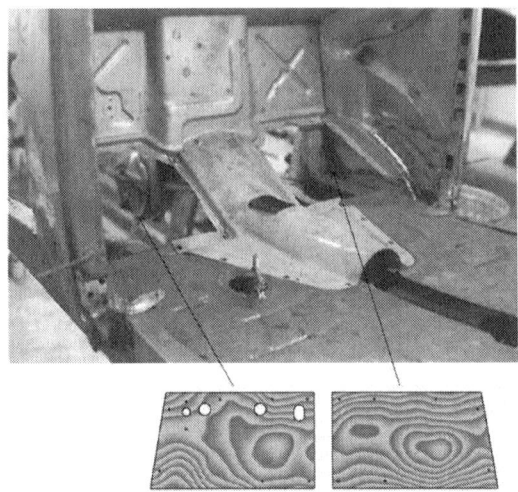

The wooden floorboards are depicted. Also, the dark-colored sections are the left and right reproduction replacement floors in primer paint. In the middle is the bolted transmission "hump." Note how clean and new-looking the sheet metal was after chemical stripping. The "hump" in the floor had yet to be fabricated. This hump, when welded in, tied both left and right sides together.[48]

Henry Ford specified that certain procured parts be shipped to his factory in wooden boxes of an odd shape. He took the box, broke it apart and reused the sides for the wooden floorboards underneath the driver and passenger feet. Now that was thrift!

Also, the rumble seat floor was shot and needed to be constructed.

On the right, rumble seat floor on the car as delivered; on the left, reconstructed rumble seat floor[49]

Entire floor welded up   The discolored left and right floor sections are actually in primer paint[50]

49

50

Rotted rear wheel-well cut-out[51]

Entire rear wheel-well from a donor car welded in-place[52]

---

51

52

This is the side view of the restored chassis in my driveway. The frame was from a 1938 Ford Sedan parts-car. The engine and transmission had not been installed as yet. The tires were original and were used to roll the chassis around. New tires were procured subsequently. Photo by Author

Author posing with restored chassis. Photo is reversed; steering should be on the left.

This photo depicts the restored rolling chassis minus engine and transmission, in my driveway. The photo was printed backwards, as the steering wheel should have been on the left side.

Milestone: Restored body mounted on restored chassis, 11/18/85. Note the old tires used to move car around[53]

Photo taken 1/30/86; this was starting to look like a car[54]

Dash and various moldings were sent out to have wood grained paint applied.[55]

---

54

55

As time went by, the restoration had progressed to the point that a restored rolling chassis was assembled in one bay of my two-car garage. The chassis consisted of a frame, suspension, gas tank, fuel lines, old tires and brakes. Next I placed the rebuilt engine onto the frame and bolted it down. The time had come to fire-off the engine for the first time. Fuel was added to the gas tank, a new six volt battery was strapped to the side of the frame, and a cup of gas was poured down the carburetor throat. The engine fired, but it would not run continuously.

Barry, from work, came by to help me one evening. He discovered that the gas tank was not feeding gas to the engine. When I had restored the tank, I used a "sloshing compound" to seal any pinholes and rust internally. What I didn't appreciate was that this compound also sealed the internal tube that fed the mating fuel line that ran to the engine. My friend managed to poke through this blockage, using a spare speedometer flex cable. Subsequent cranking of the engine resulted in it firing off. What a feeling it was to hear the engine run for the first time after all that work!

In 2011, it was time to relocate to The Villages, Florida, permanently. My son, Scott, had also purchased a house in The Villages, but had not moved from Massachusetts yet. I decided to downsize and give him my 1939 Ford convertible, with the caveat that he had to take all the spare parts that I had collected over the years. There was an additional caveat; he was not to sell the car or convert it to a hot rod, as long as I was alive. The two spare engines included in that "stash" were not used for the restoration. Scott decided that he could not justify moving the two engines to Florida, as they weighed approximately 500 pounds apiece. I advertised in the antique car circles that I was active in, to sell the engines, to no avail. Then I changed the ad to give them away for free, with no takers. I was getting desperate. I contacted a local antique Ford parts supplier, and inquired if he was interested. He told me that his cousin would take the engine assemblies off my hands, and that was the end of the spare engines.

The shop restored the body to the point the restored chassis in my garage was needed. I bartered the leftover frame from the 1941 Ford parts car for a tow of the chassis to the shop. The completely restored body and chassis were mated.

Car returned from upholstery shop.[56]

The shop needed a rumble seat release cable (flexible cable that runs within an armored outer sheath) that ran from the trunk handle to the seat release mechanism. This was not available on the restoration parts market. I was sweating out where I could locate a part like this. I thought about it for a day, and decided to try a bicycle repair shop. I figured that a bicycle handbrake cable should do the job. Sure enough, they had what I needed. I felt good about that one. Sometimes one has to win to keep the game interesting.

---

56

By the time the restoration was complete, I was into the car for approximately $25,000, including the purchase price of $1500. Since the going rate at the time, circa 1986, for a fully restored 1939 Ford Convertible Coupe Deluxe was $25,000, I could have purchased a car in Number One Condition (perfect condition, just having completed a complete restoration) from a no-rust western state for the cost of the restoration, and the car would never have been rusted. Today, with shop rates upward of $100/hour, the cost to pay someone else to restore a car is prohibitive vs. the market value. The way to purchase an antique car is to let the other guy pay for the restoration. Then, pay for a professional appraisal on the car, and make a bid accordingly. The hobbyist will be way ahead, financially.

## Trip Home from Restoration Shop

It was 1986. After two years in the restoration shop, the time came to drive the car home. The route required a leg on Interstate 95 of approximately 25 miles as well as back roads at the beginning and end of the journey. This was the maiden voyage for the completed car, and I was nervous. Initially, everything went well, but as the miles added up, the car slowed perceptibly, and the engine temperature gage showed hotter than normal. This situation became progressively worse, until I had to pull over to investigate. I noticed that my brake taillights were illuminated constantly. I let things cool down and moved out again, with the same results. After many stops, I made it home.

Investigation revealed that the hydraulic brakes were not adjusted correctly. There was a tiny bleed hole in the brake master cylinder that needed to be uncovered by the shaft from the brake pedal, to allow brake fluid to return from the wheel cylinders as the fluid got hot, with normal driving. When this hole was not open, as the fluid heated up, it expanded and basically applied the brakes. That was why the brakes came on by themselves, the brake lights lit and the engine ran hot trying to overcome the drag of the brakes.

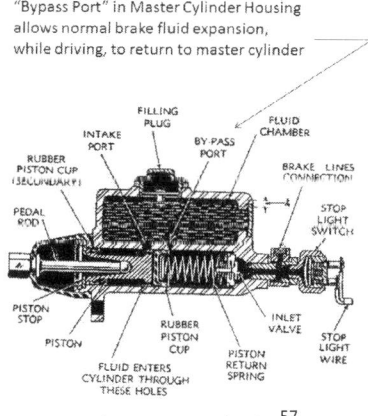

Brake Master Cylinder[57]

---

57

---

I attempted to perform a front wheel alignment using a tape measure between the front wheel front and back surfaces. Also, I sighted from the front to the rear to align the front wheels with the rears. It didn't work out, as the front tires started to wear unevenly. I took the car to a recommended shop. There was an old-timer working there, who informed me that the width of the front wheels was different than that of the rears, so that was why my amateur alignment was incorrect.

My goal was to have the car completely restored in order to attend the Eastern National Meet of The Early Ford V8 Club of America. This was scheduled for August 4-8, 1986, in Westborough, approximately 40 miles from my home in Peabody, Massachusetts. That goal was met, barely. The Early Ford V-8 Club judged the entered cars, in order to evaluate the condition as compared to the condition as it left the factory. Judging was serious business, with a 999 point system. When a Ford has been restored, the judging process is the best way to learn about the mistakes made.

The car was painted using the original Nitrocellulose Lacquer. The paint had to age before it could be buffed out, but there was not sufficient time. I drove the car the Eastern National without buffing it out. The trip was convoy style with a friend from GE who had a 1937 Ford Tudor. The event was enjoyable, and my car accumulated sufficient points during judging to garner a third place, which was respectable. The advantage of undergoing the grueling judging process was I learned what was not correct for the 1939 Ford Convertible Coupe Deluxe, as it left the factory.

During one day of the meet, I decided to fill the gas tank in anticipation of the drive home. Upon returning, I parked next to a show-car the identical model to mine, right down to the color of the paint. A while later, I returned to find that my car was not there. I started to panic, when someone informed me that my gas tank was overflowing through the filler cap. The owner of the show-car was nervous that my car might catch fire and damage his, so he pushed my car to the opposite end of the parking lot. As the outside temperature increased, the fuel in my gas tank expanded and went out the overflow. I learned to fill the tank in the afternoon or to not fill the tank completely.

The show car was identical as to make, model and color to mine. One could have eaten lunch off the engine compartment. Everything was perfect and spotless. The battery was "Ford" script and the voltage regulator had the correct cadmium plate cover. Both parts are hard to come by.

Photo by Author

My car is on the left. An acquaintance, Jon, who sold me my second 1950 Mercury (see chapter 9), parked his 1939 Ford Convertible Coupe Deluxe next to mine. His car was a survivor, but definitely not restored. Note the sealed beam headlights, which didn't come out until 1940, and the incorrect hub caps. Photo by Author

Quarter rear view; Jon's driver is on the left and my restored car is on the right.
Photo by Author

1939 Fords lined up for judging at the Eastern National Convention of the Early Ford V-8 Club of America, in August 1986. Note the 1939 Ford Standard, on the right, has a different body style from the other, Deluxe models.
Photo by Author

Open wide and say, "AHHH."
Photo by Author

Note the handsome grill and the take-apart headlight.
Photo by Author

Early showings of the Ford

I entered the Ford in my club (NSOCC) car show. While I waited for the car to be judged, a gentleman walked up to me and said, "I have been looking for this exact car. I am willing to pay you $25,000 for it." Since this was the average auction value for a 1939 Ford convertible coupe in Number One condition, I was tempted. However, I just finished the restoration, and I waivered. I told the buyer that I would consider his offer while I made a business trip for the following two days, and I would call him when I returned.

While on the road, I decided to sell the car. Upon returning, I called the man in Vermont. He told me that he located another one, and was no longer in the market. The moral of the story is, never fall in love with a car. If a decent offer is made, sell it and buy another one.

Another year, at the same car show, I returned to the parking lot where my Ford was located, and found a note on my windshield to call someone. This individual wanted to trade a 1960s Lincoln and a houseboat located in Florida for my 1939 Ford   I was not interested.

1960s Lincoln[58]

A friend (and car club member) offered to trade me his Ford Model T Roadster for my Ford. I was definitely not interested in this deal.

## Ford Flathead Engine Inherent Defect

Once I started driving the car, I learned about the inherent defect in the design of the Ford flathead V-8 engine. The exhaust gases passed through the engine block before they exited the engine. By doing so, the exhaust gases added an additional heat load to the engine cooling system that doesn't exist in other engine designs. The Ford flathead V-8 had a reputation of running hot, in its day. This resulted in a common malady called vapor lock. The fuel pump was located on top of the engine, right where the heat load was very high. At idle speed, after a hard run, when the engine was hot, the fuel would change into its vapor state rather than liquid state. The fuel pump could not "suck" vapor fuel, only liquid fuel. The engine would then simply stall, as it ran out of fuel in the carburetor.

My 1939 Ford Convertible Coupe Deluxe
Photo by Author

Dealing with the Cooling Problem
Various tricks were used to deal with the possibility of vapor lock. One was to apply wooden clothes pins along the fuel tube. The wood was a good insulator and kept the fuel in the tube cool enough to remain liquid. Another was to use a glove with ice on top of the fuel pump. Also used was a sheet metal heat shield between the hot engine and the fuel tube. This heat shield reflected approximately 50% of the heat coming up from the engine, away from the tube. Some people tried insulating the fuel tube.

The best solution was to add an electric fuel pump in series with the mechanical fuel pump. The electric pump needed to be located near the low spot of the fuel line from the gas tank; the pump worked by pushing fuel rather than sucking.

I had driven my Ford to an assembly point for an old-car cruise, and shut the engine off while I schmoozed for a while. It was time to move out; all the other cars took off and my Ford wouldn't start. By the time I got it running, it was too late to catch up with the others. I subsequently retrofitted an electric fuel pump in series with the mechanical fuel pump, in order to make my car more reliable. This pump was wired through an under-dash switch, so I could control when to use the extra pump. Normally, the electric pump was shut off. However, when the car encountered conditions where it ran hot, I simply turned on the electric fuel pump.

Various remedies have been tried to overcome the inherent cooling problem with the Ford flathead V-8 engine. One method was to "rod out" the radiator core. The top tank of the radiator was removed by a radiator shop by unsoldering the joint, and an appropriate sized rod was gently forced down the individual core tubes to remove any deposits that tend to clog the flow of coolant.

Another remedy was to substitute higher flow water pumps on the engine. Skip Haney of Punta Gorda, Florida remanufactures the stock Ford water pump to increase the water flow by 50%, by changing the impeller design. I have these improved water pumps on the Ford.

Some hobbyists have removed the thermostats from the upper radiator hoses. This could cause more problems that it solved, as short trips in cooler weather will result in the engine not heating up to operating temperature, and the formation of sludge in the engine oil. The proper size thermostats should not cause overheating.

A six volt electric cooling fan is available for retrofit on old Fords. The fan is controlled by a thermostatic switch. I never purchased one, but I understand this is effective in keeping the coolant temperature under control. The only disadvantage is that it does not look correct for the 1939 Ford.

### Is it Vapor Lock or an Overheated Coil Failure?
There is a school of thought indicating vapor lock wasn't the problem; rather the coil insulation between the windings in the ignition coil overheated and shorted out. When the engine cooled down, the insulation restored itself and the coil performed as designed. I suspect that both issues were in play at various times.

### Sticky Valves in the Flathead V-8
Now is the time to put in a plug for Marvel Mystery Oil. Use a cap full of Marvel Mystery Oil in the gas tank, and sticky valves should not be a problem. Consult the early ford v-8 forum for multiple testimonials about the use of this lubricant. The following is quoted from the Marvel Mystery Oil website:

"Marvel Mystery Oil is completely safe in today's high-tech cars and provide the same benefits as it has since 1923-cleaner engines, upper cylinder lubrication, reduced acid and sludge build up, improved fuel economy, clean and lubricated fuel systems and many more!"[59]

I have no direct evidence about the beneficial effects of the oil, but I have gleaned information from many antique car owners who verify the beneficial effects of the use.

---

59

## A Couple of Dumb Ideas in the 1939 Ford Design
Headlight Switch

The headlight switch is located at the base of the steering column. This is just where all the dirt and moisture collected while the car was being driven. The switch is held in place by a spring that is difficult to remove and more difficult to replace. There is a trick to this procedure, but a visit to an old time mechanic may be necessary to learn it.

Speedometer Gear

The gear that drives the speedometer cable, and, subsequently, the speedometer is located on the driveshaft. Unfortunately, the driveshaft is located within the torque tube and is not accessible from the outside. I experienced a failure of this drive gear. Initially, I experienced a squeaking noise followed by a failure of the speedometer. A friend offered to help me replace this gear. The car needed to be jacked up, the transmission cover removed from the floor of the car, topside. Then, from beneath the car, the torque tube had to be unbolted, the brakes disconnected and the rear springs disconnected from the car. In short, this was a **bastard** of a job. All this to replace a simple speedometer gear!

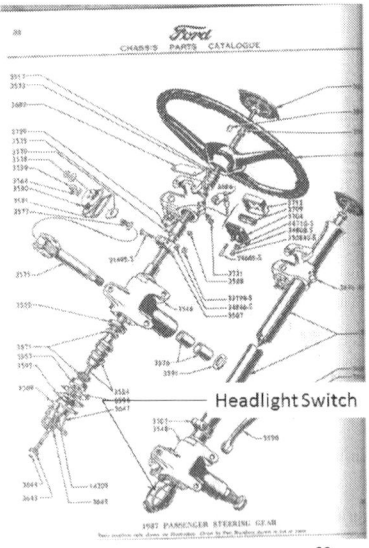

Location of Headlight Switch[60]

Speedometer Gear inside torque tube

Location of Speedometer Gear[61]

## Year of Manufacture License Plate

Massachusetts passed a law allowing the year-of-manufacture license plate on an antique car. In other words, if I found an original 1939 license plate, I could register my 1939 Ford with this plate. It had to be original, not restored. There was one caveat. If someone had another year license plate with the same number, the Registry would not allow the duplicate plate.

[61]

An acquaintance of mine in the NSOCC sold his collection of original Massachusetts antique license plates. He had a very nice plate from 1939, and I bought it for $20. My insurance company made out the paperwork, and I went to the Registry. The clerk saw the plate and was excited about the quality of the old plate. She called her supervisor over, and they both fawned over it for a while. Then the clerk looked up the number, and found that another club member in Peabody, Massachusetts had the same number, but in a later year. They wouldn't allow the registration.

My original license plate from 1939 sits on a pegboard in my garage. The Registry of Motor Vehicles would not allow me to register the Ford with this number. Photo by Author

## My Problem with the Massachusetts Department of Revenue

I purchased the car as an incomplete collection of corroded and distressed parts. At the time, I didn't feel that it was necessary to pay the automobile sales tax on the "junk." However, once the car was restored, several years later, I was faced with the need to confess my omission to the Department of Revenue of Massachusetts. I was supposed to pay sales tax on the "car" within seven days of the purchase. The personnel at the state sales tax office were not pleased, and intended to penalize me. I was able to reconstruct the sales tax I paid for all the parts I purchased within the state during the restoration, because I saved every receipt. I submitted the documentation and the state accepted it, with a small penalty, which I paid. I really sweated that one out.

## Problem with the Ignition Switch

One lesson learned during the restoration was if I reused a part without restoring it, this part bit me in the butt later on. The prime example was the ignition switch. This part was a take-apart unit that mounted on the back of the steering column. The switch looked OK so I reused it. Once I started driving my car, it had the nasty habit of quitting expectantly. If I waited for a while, the car started normally. I returned from a car meet one evening around dusk. While transitioning from US Route 1 to a secondary road, and negotiated a curved ramp, the engine quit. I pulled over as far as I could, but was exposed, as cars coming around the curving ramp could not see me until the last moment.

I stood behind my car, waving my flashlight to warn off other cars coming around the curve. Finally, a car with teenagers stopped to help. They waved the cars around me with my flashlight while I "hot-wired" the ignition switch, on a lark, and the engine fired off immediately. Son of a gun, the switch was bad. Later, when I had a chance to take apart the switch, the Bakelite insulator was cracked. The ignition voltage heated the carbon tracks in the crack to the point that the voltage shorted to ground, thereby killing the engine ignition.

This part had a crack in the bakelite. As the part heated up with operation, the ignition power shorted to ground, killing to ignition to the engine

 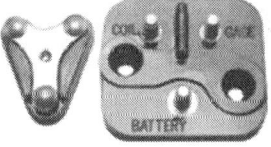

Ignition Switch for my 1939 Ford, Exploded View

Exploded view of the ignition switch for my 1939 Ford.[62]

62

Ignition switch, view from the driver's seat
Photo by Author

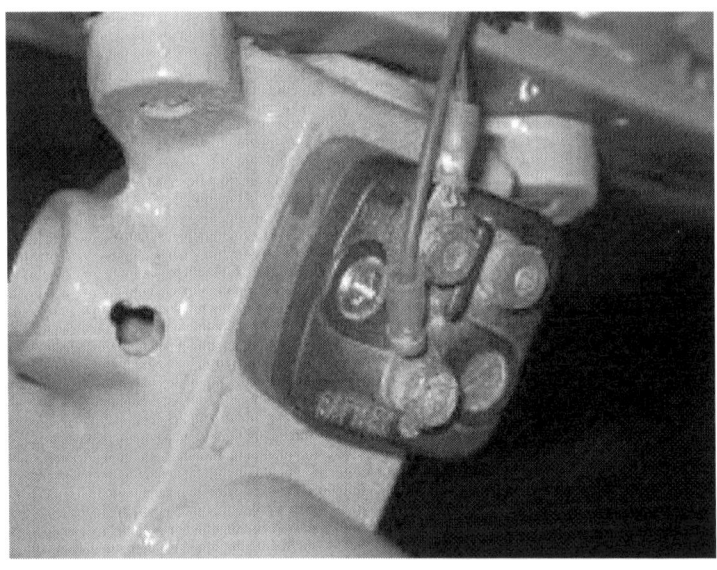

Ignition switch, view from the rear, behind the steering column
Photo by Author

Ford Flathead Ignition Coils

One problem area discovered during the restoration was the Ford flathead ignition coil. Original coils that actually work are difficult to locate. This coil is located on the front of the engine, on top of the distributor, where the heat load is greatest. Long term exposure to excessive heat tends to break down the insulation between the coil windings. The part looked normal, and may even work when the engine was cool, but stopped working when it was hot. When I started my restoration, there was one reproduction ignition coil on the market, and it was manufactured in Argentina. The part had a poor record for reliability. I bought one, and, sure enough, it failed fairly quickly.

An alternative came on the market. It utilized a modern six-volt coil with an adapter kit. The modern coil mounted remotely in the engine compartment, where it was cool, such as on an inner fender well. The adapter kit and modern six volt coil worked satisfactorily, but looked out of place, and definitely was not original-looking. I limped along with this setup for some time, until there was a better alternative.

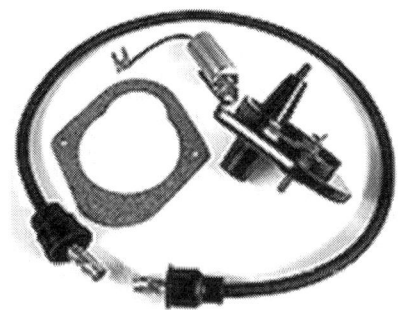

Adapter Kit for Modern Six Volt Coil       Modern Six Volt Ignition Coil

Modern Six Volt Coil with Adapter[63]

---

63

Skip Haney developed a procedure to drill out the rivets of the original coil, clean out the guts, and replace the internals with a modern six-volt coil. The assembly then was riveted back together and the coil was as new, with no outward looking changes. I purchased one of these, and have been happy with the part performance.

Original Ford Flathead Dual-Point Distributor and Coil. Photo by Author

I attended a big car show at the Endicott Estates in Dedham, Massachusetts, one July, in the middle of a heat wave. This show was located about a one-hour drive on Interstate 95 South. I left home early to avoid the peak temperature of the day. When I arrived, after a hard drive, there was a line of antique cars wrapped around the entire block. I crawled forward slowly, while watching the coolant temperature gage. When it peaked out at 220 degrees, I stopped and raised the engine hood. I continued to crawl by looking around the raised hood. By the time I was at the head of the line, I saw the problem. The show sponsors were collecting an admission fee, and they had the old cars in a precariously imminent-overheat condition. When I got to the admission taker, I just drove past, I was so upset.

On the ride home, down I95 North, the ambient temperature was already in the 90s. The car started bucking as it was starved for fuel (incipient vapor lock). I switched on the electric fuel pump and drove home without experiencing complete vapor lock.

I attended a car meet, and parked the Ford in the "Car Corral." I enjoyed the antique car flea market for the rest of the morning, and returned to my car after 11:00 A.M. to eat my lunch. I sat in the Ford when two elderly gentlemen walked past and one commented to the other, "Look, even the clock works." I looked, and the clock was stopped at 11:20. It was 11:20 A.M., but the clock was not working. What a coincidence. Even a broken clock is correct twice a day!

The day came for me to "show" the car for the first time. The function was the annual car show weekend for my club, the NSOCC. I entered the car for judging on the Sunday morning of the weekend. The car took a third place in its category, which wasn't bad for the first time out. Several months later, at the club banquet, I sat at a table of club members who I did not know. One member talked about the 1939 Ford convertible coupe that had "every modification known to man." I was embarrassed, but I knew that this man didn't know I owned the car of interest. I guess the reason he made that comment was I had the following non-standard parts:


Non-split core radiator
> I elected not to re-core the radiator with a split-core radiator because of cost.

Electric fuel pump
> I needed the electric fuel pump for improved reliability in hot weather.

Modern six volt coil with an adapter kit
> There was not a source of reliable original Ford coils.

Trafficators
> I elected to retain these European directional signals.

I am sure that someone pulled him aside and told him that the owner of the car was at his table. He did not apologize.

Restored Massachusetts 1939 License Plate

Take-Apart Headlight

The restored Massachusetts license plate is for show, only. The car was registered with an antique plate on the rear, from Massachusetts. Note the WWII ration "A" sticker on the upper passenger windshield.

Photo by Author

## Tour to Nova Scotia

I was active in the NSOCC. A tour was planned to Nova Scotia, one summer. I was nervous about going that far in an antique car, but agreed to go. The plan was to drive to South Portland, Maine, load the car onto the overnight ferry, The Scotia Prince, and board.

But first I had to drive to Portland, Maine. I agreed to rendezvous with two other antique cars in Georgetown, about 10:00 A.M. Then we moved out, convoy style, towards Portland. As I was tail gunner, more often than not, when the convoy approached a traffic light, I didn't make it through before it changed to red. I didn't care, I sailed right through. I gambled that any law enforcement officer would be more interested in looking at my old Ford that at the yellow or red light. I had no problems, but I sweated it out.

The ferry docked in Yarmouth, Nova Scotia the next morning. All went well and we had fun touring southern Nova Scotia. We made a trip to a private car collection in Plymouth, Nova Scotia and were driving back to our hotel in Yarmouth.

I followed a friend in his Ford Model A. Suddenly, he made a panic stop on the soft shoulder of the highway, and I followed suit right behind him. As I came to a stop, my brakes didn't feel right. I asked him if everything was all right, and he replied that someone else was following him back, and he lost sight of the other car in his rear view mirror.

From that time onwards, my brakes were spongy. I observed a slight seepage on one of the front wheel brake cylinders, so I knew that I had to be careful while using the brakes for the rest of the trip. I kept adding brake fluid to the master brake cylinder to keep the fluid level where it needed to be. We were in Nova Scotia the weekend that JF Kennedy Jr. was killed while piloting a private plane to Hyannis, Massachusetts, along with his wife and others. We watched the news on TV in our hotel room.

Ford Model A Coupe, similar to the one owned by a fellow car club member. Photo by Author

My 1939 Ford in Nova Scotia
Photo by Author

The Scotia Prince[64]

On the return trip, after we unloaded our cars off the ferry in South Portland, Maine, I asked one of my friends, who had a 1941 Lincoln Convertible, and who lived in the next town, to follow me home on the highway, in case I had a problem with the brakes. Except for a complete stop at a toll booth, where I had to use the hand brake, everything was uneventful. I was able to repair the brakes once I got home.

Event at the USS Constitution
The NSOCC had an event at the USS Constitution in Charlestown, Massachusetts, a suburb of Greater Boston. It was a particularly hot Sunday. We were all huddled in the shade under a picnic area canopy, eating our lunch. The antique cars were parked in a row where the public could see them. Suddenly, a tour bus pulled up and discharged a group of Japanese tourists. Before I knew it, there was a tourist sitting in my car, posing, while another tourist took his picture. I walked up to the one in the driver's seat, and asked him what he was doing sitting in my car. He was very embarrassed; he thought the cars were part of a museum display and wanted a picture taken.

The author is driving his 1939 Ford Convertible in a parade in Marblehead, Massachusetts. Photo by Author

## Unwitting experience with a radiator pressure cap

I decided to add a pressure cap to my radiator in order to raise the boiling point of the engine coolant. What I did not know was that the overboard drain tube had been welded shut by a previous owner. I participated in a Patriots Day Parade and returned home, frustrated with the Ford's poor cooling system under parade conditions. I parked the car in one bay of my two-bay garage and went into my house. About 10 minutes later, while upstairs, I heard a noise that sounded like a "thunk." I returned to the garage and observed engine coolant all over the floor and engine bay.

The pressure had built up in the cooling system, and instead of being relieved by the pressure cap and flowing overboard, the pressure was trapped. It got to the point where the radiator hose on one side of the engine simply blew off its interfacing gooseneck on the engine head. The solution was to cutoff the drain tube and fit a rubber hose vented to the atmosphere.

## Parade in Cambridge, Massachusetts

Another friend asked me to participate in a parade in Cambridge, Massachusetts, to commemorate Portuguese Day. I had magnetic signs on my two doors and Miss Portugal sitting on my rumble seat. This sounded like a good idea, and I agreed even though the location was somewhat out of my area. Everything went according to plan as we were directed to our location in the parade sequence. As it progressed, we stopped at every cross street for an unknown reason, and waited until the movement reinitiated. I need to mention that the Ford flathead engine needed to move at a speed of at least five to seven miles hour to aid in cooling through the radiator, or I was in trouble.

The parade continued for two hours while we made innumerable stops at cross streets. The engine temperature gage showed that the cooling system was definitely upset with the slow progress. Finally, I knew the end of the parade was around the corner and down one more street.

We were barely moving, and I started to smell the sweet odor of radiator coolant as it expanded out the radiator overflow onto the street. The temperature gage was all the way to "220F."

I made a command decision, and pulled off to the side of the road, shut off the engine and raised the hood to aid in cooling the engine down. I turned to Miss Portugal and said, "Miss Portugal, you will have to find a ride for the rest of the parade." Luckily, the modern car in front of mine had her parents as passengers, so she was able to make the transition easily. As my car was parked, cooling off, a friend in his 1965 Mustang convertible crawled by and suddenly threw up his engine coolant all over the engine and street. I guess I stopped just in time. I was definitely unhappy with parades. It was no fun when I watched the engine temperature gage, while damning the slow progress of a parade.

## GE Sponsored Car Show

My employer, GE, sponsored a car show. The participants were asked to come in period costume. I purchased a WWII Army Air Corps uniform from an "Army/Navy Store" and rented a flight jacket from a costume store. I applied my retired Air Force rank and added my wings. Marilyn purchased a period outfit at a vintage clothing store. I took a third prize in the people's choice contest.

GR Dornfeld and Marilyn pose in period costume for the GE car show
Photo by Author

## A Hooker and Her Pimp

I attended a cruise night at a local shopping center, in Danvers, Massachusetts, when I spotted two unusual looking individuals walking across the parking lot from the shopping center to the lot for the collector cars. Something didn't look right. The woman was African American, looked about 20 years old, and was dressed to the hilt with a long slinky dress and a slit all the way up to her hips. She was accompanied by a much older Caucasian man, perhaps seventy years old, wearing shorts and sneakers.

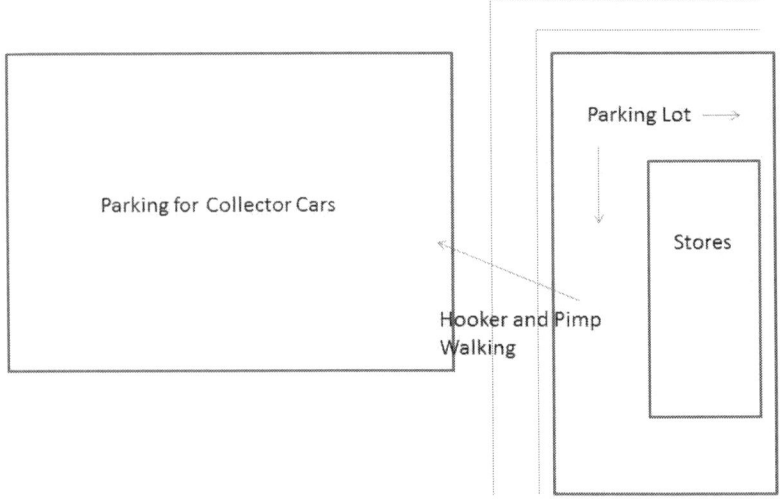

Parking for Collector Cars

Parking Lot ⟶

Stores

Hooker and Pimp Walking

Sketch by Author

The scene just didn't compute.  When they entered the parking area for our cars, they passed out business cards.  She was a hooker and he was her pimp.  This went on for a while, until the Danvers Police arrived.  The two officers must have responded to a cell phone call. The police officers took the two entrepreneurs to the side and talked to them for a considerable amount of time.  I actually lost interest.  I think the officers attempted to move the entrepreneurs off the property, peacefully, and they were arguing.  That was the first and last time I ever saw a hooker at a car show.  Maybe I live a protected life.

Interesting People with Misinformation
I met the most interesting people.  At a cruise-in, a man approached me and told me that my car was incorrect.  He said it was supposed to have a crank–out windshield.  Actually, he was only partially correct.  All the 1939 Fords had crank-out windshields, except for the convertibles and the "woodie" wagons.

At another cruise-in, a man told me that he used to reach back from the driver's seat and pull the convertible top up over his head. Since he was adamant, I let him believe that story. Actually, I can barely push the convertible top up from the "down" position, when I am standing, much less pull it up over my head.

Another man told me that he first had sex in the rumble seat of the 1939 Ford. If that was the case, he must have been much smaller back then, because there is very little room.

### Original Owner's Manual for 1939 Ford Deluxe

I attended an antique car flea market, and talked to a vendor from whom I purchased many parts, via mail order. He remembered me by saying, "Oh, yes, you are the one with the Danish 1937 Ford Convertible." I refreshed his memory by saying that, actually, I had a 1939 Ford Convertible from Denmark. Just then, a stranger behind me said, "Do you own a 1939 Ford Deluxe?" I replied in the affirmative. He said that his dad had one, and that he had the original owner's manual in a desk in his attic. If I would give him my name and address, he would send it to me. I did as he requested, but thought as soon as he left, he would forget about it.

The next Tuesday, a package was in my mail box with the owner's manual. I was thrilled beyond belief, as this manual was not being reproduced. The owner's manual for the Ford Standard model was available reproduction, but not the Deluxe. I sent photographs of my car to this gentleman with a hearty thank you.

### Original Gas Ration Sticker from WWII

A friend in the NSOCC came across a box of original WWII ration stickers. I purchased one for my Ford for a nominal $1.

Ration Sticker on the upper RH windshield of my car.
Photo by Author

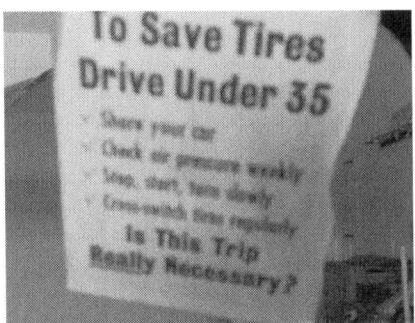

Back of my ration sticker

Original Owner's Manual for the 1939 Ford Deluxe

This manual is not being reproduced, so my ability to locate one was a real "find."[65]

Enjoying the Old Car:

There were many reasons to join an old-car club, but driving the car while enjoying the camaraderie was the best. Some of the meets I attended were as follows:

- Nursing Home visits, where the patients reminisced and voted for their favorite car
- Local Community Public Displays
- Arts & Crafts Shows
- Mystery Tours in the evening
- Picnics
- Overnight Tours, such as our trip to Nova Scotia
- Cruise-ins at the local parking lots

65

In many areas, one could go to a different cruise-in, virtually every night in the summer.

- Parades:       Some old cars had no problem with engine cooling.  However, Fords were susceptible to overheating.  There was an annual July 4th parade in a North Shore community, where the NSOCC was invited to attend.  We were promised that the old cars would lineup right behind the parade-leading fire engines.  This worked out for many years, until, one year, the Parade Marshal reneged on the promise.  The old cars were placed behind marching cub scouts and camp fire girls.  After sweating out the old Ford's cooling, that was the last parade I attended.

- Technical Meets       The NSOCC had a Technical Meet once a month, on Sunday morning, throughout the driving season.  The meet was scheduled at a house, where there was ample parking, and an automotive subject was discussed.  Coffee and donuts were served.  The meet broke up before noon, so the day could be enjoyed with the family.  These meets were enjoyable and I always learned something.

I was active in the NSOCC for many years.  I ran for Board of Directors three times, but was not elected, primarily because I was not known to the membership. Meanwhile, the monthly newsletter had deteriorated under the stewardship of the then-current editor, and when this man wanted to relinquish the role, I volunteered.  I then turned the newsletter into a first-class monthly document.  I performed as the editor for eight years.

By then, I was known to the membership, and successfully ran for the offices of President, Vice President, and Secretary, as well as Board of Directors.  The only post I did not occupy was Treasurer, because I simply didn't want the responsibility.

# Private Car Collection[66]

The NSOCC was active, with approximately 30 meets per year. One notable meet was the trip to a private museum, in August 2003. This museum was located in Newbury, Massachusetts, where the owner employed a staff of antique auto mechanics and auto body experts. The museum was not open to the public, except by invitation. In his collection, the owner had one of every Ford flathead V-8 engine-powered car made. The years ran from 1932 through 1953. He had convertibles, station wagons (woodies), sedans and trucks from every year. His cars were perfect. There wasn't a ding in any body and the paint was flawless. In his museum he had many collectables, such as motor-oil lighted signs, auto marque lighted signs, spare engines painted as new, and so forth. His staff was gracious to serve coffee and donuts to his guests.

1936 Ford Convertible in the collection
Photo by Author

In the pecking order of collectability, convertibles were the most in demand, followed by "Woody" station wagons, coupes, and then, way down on the list, sedans.

---

66

This car was the same make and model as mine, a 1939 Ford Convertible Coupe Deluxe, except that the owner's car was perfect. Note the double whitewall tires which were correct for the car. Photo by Author

1940 Lincoln Zephyr Convertible. These cars were particularly attractive, no thanks to Henry Ford. His son, Edsel Ford, was responsible for the gorgeous body design. Henry was dead set against frills. Photo by Author.

1950 Ford Convertible.  Note the memorabilia on display.  Photo by Author

Note the Woodies and trucks on the second level, with convertibles on the ground floor.
Photo by Author

The club then convoyed to the owner's '50s Diner located nearby. The diner had been purchased whole, was broken down for shipment and reassembled on-site. His staff hired a caterer to flip hamburgers and fries, to order, in his diner while we listened to music from the period. As we drove up to his property, a photographer took a picture of each car in front of his diner. Before the day was out, the photo was developed and presented to each car owner.

A club member had just completed his restoration of a post-war Ford convertible, and the car kept stalling for lack of fuel. He needed to get the "bugs" out of the car. Photo by Author

My 1939 Ford Convertible Coupe Deluxe parked in front of the 50s diner.[67]

## Parts of Foreign Manufacture

I took part in a static display at an assisted living facility in Peabody. When it was time to go home, the car would not start. Subsequent investigation revealed that the "Chinese made" ignition points developed a crack in the plastic portion, such that the points did not open when the distributor cam called for it. My mechanic friend substituted some original Ford stock he had hanging around his shop. Beware of Chinese-made parts. Actually, beware of any foreign made parts. The best option is to locate original Ford-made parts, even if they are used.

---

[67]

Dual Point Distributor

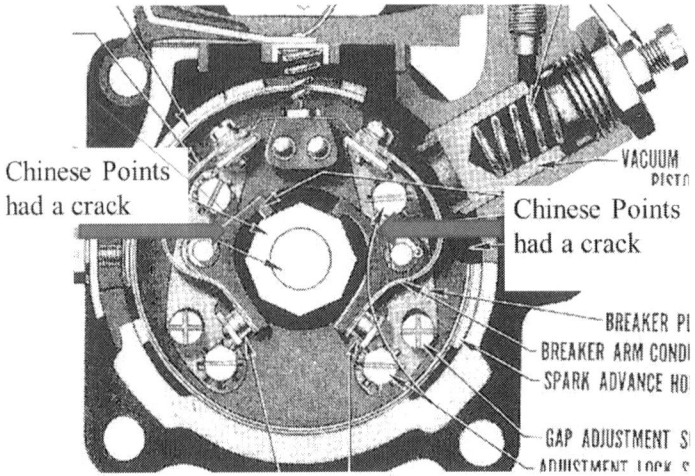

Chinese Points had a crack

Chinese Points had a crack

VACUUM PISTO

BREAKER PI
BREAKER ARM CONDI
SPARK ADVANCE HO

GAP ADJUSTMENT S
ADJUSTMENT LOCK S

The distributor cam opened the breaker point, but the crack prevented
The points from actually opening

View of the ignition distributor internals[68]

## Driving my old Ford

In my opinion, driving the old Ford is the most enjoyable aspect of the hobby. Once the newness of the restoration wore off, it didn't make sense to enter the car at car shows strictly for trophies, as opposed to driving it. My experience is that driving the car on Saturdays is more dangerous than on Sundays. On Saturday, people are buzzing about trying to get shopping out of the way quickly, and they do not pay much attention to an old car that is being driven defensively. Sunday is a completely different story. Drivers are more relaxed. However, be cautious when driving on a highway.

---

I can't relate how many times I have been passed by a modern car, and, just as it comes beside me, the driver looks over and beeps his horn. That is to tell me I am driving an old car. Heck, I knew that. Then comes the dangerous part.

As the driver looks to his right, at me, he instinctively biases the steering wheel in the direction he is looking, and his modern car starts to encroach into my lane. I can't tell you how many times this has happened. Now, when I encounter that situation, I back off in speed to make sure the modern car doesn't hit my Ford.

Gasoline with 10% Ethanol
Currently, every service station is pumping gas with a blend of 10% ethanol. This has been an unmitigated disaster for the antique car hobby. Ethanol is distilled from fermented corn. The unintended consequences of 10% ethanol have been severe for my hobby. The primary problem with this blend of gasoline is ethanol is hydroscopic (will absorb water). It is also an excellent solvent (dissolves plastic, rubber, fiberglass and more).

Due to ethanol's affinity for water, phase separation and water contamination occur quickly. Modern cars utilize materials that are not affected by ethanol

My experience with ethanol in the 1939 Ford was premature replacement of the gas tank, fuel tube from the tank to the firewall, the rubber fuel hose to the fuel pump, the mechanical fuel pump and carburetor. In other words, my son Scott and I have had to replace **every component** in the fuel system. I also had to replace the electric fuel pump twice. All the spare parts I accumulated, that are whetted by fuel, are now obsolete and cannot be used. I had several carburetor rebuild kits that are worthless, except for some metal parts, such as fuel metering jets and fasteners.

## Steel Fuel Tube from Gas Tank to Firewall

As I said, I changed every part in the fuel system whetted by 10% ethanol fuel, except the steel tube that ran from the gas tank to the firewall; I decided to finish the job. I no longer had a set of ramps, and decided to have the job performed by a NAPA Service Center. My gas gauge was not accurate below one-half full, but I did my best to minimize the fuel level in the tank to make the job easier.

The NAPA Service Center had the Ford on their lift, and invited me to act as a consultant on the job, which I appreciated. NAPA did a good job and sent me on my way. Before I left the shop, I inquired as to the distance to the nearest gas station. It was only about ¾ of a mile. I set off fat, dumb and happy, and conked out about ¼ mile from the gas station. I hoofed it back to NAPA. The manager took a gas can and his pickup truck and drove to where my Ford dead-indian awaited. He didn't even charge me for the gas, which I appreciated.

## Late Flash

As I am writing this book, a new Marathon service station just opened in my neighborhood, and has "recreational gas" or gasoline without ethanol. It is available in 90 octane, only, and retails for about $.90 cents per gallon more than 87 octane with 10% ethanol. Also, I noticed that a Chevron gas station in Leesburg, Florida has a small sign that advertises it sells non-ethanol gas.

I don't care about the price, as long as I can purchase it. Now, I don't have to worry about the gas going bad.

My restored 1939 Ford Convertible Coupe Deluxe at a car show at Topsfield Fairgrounds. Photo by Author

## Engine oil as well as gasoline is a problem for old cars[69]

Under new government emission control regulations, the anti-wear additive ZDDP (zincdialkyl-dithiophosphate for those of you that care) and a related family of similar zinc-salt additives (ZnDTP or ZDP and others) are being severely reduced in the newest passenger car oil so that the zinc and phosphorus will not damage new catalytic converters.

Testing by several engine component manufacturers revealed that older engines experience a short period of time during engine start-up where critical lubrication is insufficient between metal-to-metal lubrication points when using modern oils with reduced ZDDP/ZDTP[70].

---

69

70

The answer for older cars is to use motor oil with restored levels of ZDDP/ZDTP. The classic car owner has to be careful and do the research to make sure the motor oil is compatible with the needs of the older engine designs. There are several oils on the market that advertise adequate levels of this additive.

### Maintaining your antique car

Once I finished with the restoration, I was determined to perform as much of the routine maintenance as I could. The first task was to locate an original or reproduction service manual for the 1939 Ford. At the same time, I purchased a color-coded wiring diagram for the car. There are vendors who specialize in retailing these manuals. The best source for these vendors is in the monthly Hemmings Motor News, available at most bookstores on the magazine rack. Once I was familiar with this manual, it was time to accumulate some basic tools.

### Battery Charger

Antique cars sit most of their life in the garage. This is not healthy for the battery, as it will discharge gradually over time, and incur a condition called "Sulfation." I purchased a trickle charger and connected it to the battery at all times when the car was not in use. This insured that the battery was fully charged when I was about to take the car out.

What is sulfation[71]? During use, small sulfate crystals form, but these are normal and are not harmful. During prolonged charge deprivation, however, the amorphous lead sulfate converts to a stable crystalline that deposits on the negative plates. This leads to the development of large crystals, which reduce the battery's active material that is responsible for high capacity and low resistance. Sulfation also lowers charge acceptance. Sulfation charging will take longer because of elevated internal resistance.

### Engine Compression Tester

An engine compression tester was a must. There is little you can do to improve the way an old car is running if the engine has poor or uneven compression. The procedure is simple:

- Remove all the spark plugs

---

- Ground the power lead from the ignition coil to the distributor, at the distributor end.
- Draw a diagram of the top of the engine to record the compression value.
- Insert the tester into the spark plug hole and exercise moderate pressure to keep the tester inserted, while you crank the engine for several revolutions until the dial indicator on the tester no longer increases. Record the compression value.
- Repeat this for all the cylinders. The compression should be within 10% of each other. If not, there will need to be some mechanical repair, internally, before anything can be done on the outside of the engine to make it run better.

Front of the engine

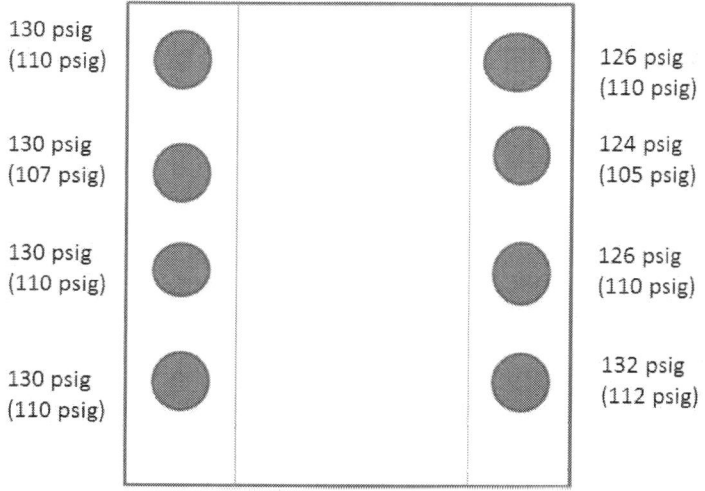

130 psig
(110 psig)

130 psig
(107 psig)

130 psig
(110 psig)

130 psig
(110 psig)

126 psig
(110 psig)

124 psig
(105 psig)

126 psig
(110 psig)

132 psig
(112 psig)

View of engine top looking down

I conducted an engine compression test after I completed reassembly of my flathead V-8. The upper value was taken before the engine was run, on 10/28/84. The value in parenthesis was obtained after five hours of running, on 6/7/85.

## Engine Vacuum/Fuel Pump Tester

Once engine compression is satisfactory, the next most valuable tool is a combination vacuum/fuel pump test gage.

Disconnect the vacuum hose between the intake manifold and windshield wiper motor, at the windshield wiper motor end. Insert the vacuum gage into this hose. Start the engine and adjust the carburetor idle speed within specs. Then, adjust the two carburetor mixture screws for the highest vacuum level on the gage.

If the engine is running poorly, there is a chart outlining the indications of the vacuum gage vs. the probable mechanical problem.

Combination Vacuum Gage and Fuel Pump Pressure Gage
Photo by Author

# Vacuum Gauge Reading

### PERTAINING TO MOTOR TUNE-UP

DARK NEEDLE INDICATES STEADY HAND
LIGHT NEEDLE INDICATES FLUCTUATING HAND

| *Normal Motor* | *Normal Motor* | *Poor Rings or Oil* | *Poor Rings or Oil* |
|---|---|---|---|
| | | 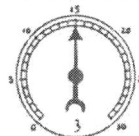 |  |
| 1 | 2 | 3 | 4 |
| Hand steady be-tween 17 and 21 | Opening and closing throttle rapidly. Rings and valves O.K. | Hand steady but lower than normal | Opening and closing throttle rapidly. Hand pulls down to zero |

| *Sticky Valve* | *Burnt Valve* | *Leaky Valve* | *Loose Valve Guides* |
|---|---|---|---|
| | 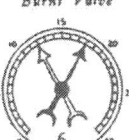 |  | 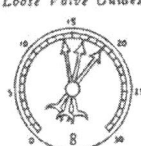 |
| 5 | 6 | 7 | 8 |
| Hand drops occa-sionally about 4 di-visions | Hand drops regular-ly several divisions | Hand drops 3 or more divisions when valve should close | Fast vibration of hand between 14 and 19 |

| *Weak Valve Springs* | *Late Valve Timing* | *Late Ignition Timing* | *Plug Gaps too Close or Points not Synchronized* |
|---|---|---|---|
|  |  |  | 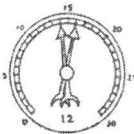 |
| 9 | 10 | 11 | 12 |
| Motor racing, hand registers 10 to 22. Wider variations as speed is increased | Hand reads from 8 to 15 and remains steady | Hand reads from 14 to 17 and remains fairly steady | Hand floats slowly between 14 and 16 |

| *Leaky Intake or Carburetor Gasket* | *Leaky Head Gasket Between Cylinders* | *Choked Muffler* | *Carburetor Out of Adjustment* |
|---|---|---|---|
|  |  |  | 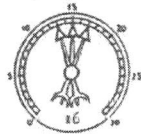 |
| 13 | 14 | 15 | 16 |
| Hand reads below 5 | Hands float regular-ly between 5 and 19 | High reading at first. Breaks to 0 and builds back slowly to about 16 | Hand floats slowly between 13 and 17 |

The engine vacuum gage reading is an invaluable tool in evaluation of the engine health.[72]

---

72

This gage can be connected to the discharge of the mechanical fuel pump. Crank the engine over with the starter and note the fuel pump discharge pressure. It should be 1 to 2 ½ psig, but no more than 5 psig.

Where do I buy parts?
Internal Engine and Transmission Parts.
These are the easiest parts to locate. There are several sources that have either New-Old-Stock (NOS), New-Old-Replacement-Stock (NORS), used or reproduction parts. Again, consult Hemmings Motor News. If you are going to get deep into an engine or transmission repair, you are advised to let a professional do the work, and he will know where to obtain the parts. Surprisingly, many parts are still available from automobile parts stores, such as NAPA. I found most of my brake system hardware there as well as the oil filter cartridge, which fits a variety of cars.

Fuel System
Every part in the fuel system is available, either reproduction or in kit form where you can renew the component. New gas tanks can be purchased, as well as "sloshing compound" to coat the internal surfaces of your old tank to seal rust or pinhole leakage paths. Carburetor rebuild kits as well as new carburetors are available. With the advent of ethanol in the gas, I would recommend that a carburetor shop rebuild your carburetor with ethanol resistant components.

The same goes for mechanical fuel pumps. You can rebuild your own with an ethanol resistant kit of parts, send it to a rebuilder or buy a new one.

Electrical System
Take your old generator to a shop specializing in generator rebuilding. I would let the experts do the work. Simple parts, such as headlight bulbs are readily available.

The purchase of a color coded wiring diagram for your car is invaluable. The electrical systems in old cars are not that complicated, and, with a little common sense, many electrical problems can be solved.

The old Fords through 1955 had a 6 volt positive-ground electrical system. Many cars of the same era had negative-ground. If it is necessary to jump start a 6 volt positive ground system with a battery incorporating negative ground, do not be confused. The battery doesn't care whether it is grounded at the positive or negative post. Simply apply the jumper cables "plus to plus" and "negative to negative." Also, when using a 12 volt battery to jump start a 6 volt system, do the same connection, only keep the jumper cables connected for a minimum time to accomplish the start. If the 12 volts are applied for too long a time, some of the light bulbs may burn out.

### AAA Roadside Service
Sooner or later, you will need a tow. Membership in AAA or any of the other roadside services will provide peace of mind. When needed, request a ramp truck so that the car will be winched up onto the ramp instead of towing your car with the front end in the air. Sooner or later, you will need their services.

### eBay
Start scanning eBay for spare parts for your car. Over time, you will accumulate a considerable supply of parts. You never know when a part is going to be required. If you are restoring a car, do not sell any spare parts until the restoration is completed. Even then, I would maintain a spare parts "store."

When I was restoring my Ford, eBay didn't exist. I attended many antique car flea markets looking for parts. Part of the fun was the adventure of the "hunt." Alas, eBay has taken that fun away. On a positive note, however, the process of looking for a specific part is more efficient.

### Unforeseen Surprises
After I gave the Ford to Scott, he encountered an unusual failure. He was driving when he noticed that the car was slowing and the coolant temperature was rising. The car forced a stop by the side of the road. The transmission experienced an internal failure such that the drivetrain locked up.

The car couldn't be moved. Unfortunately, $4000 later, the car had a completely rebuilt transmission. The transmission that failed was the one I purchased at a flea market years earlier, from a 1936 Ford. Nothing lasts forever.

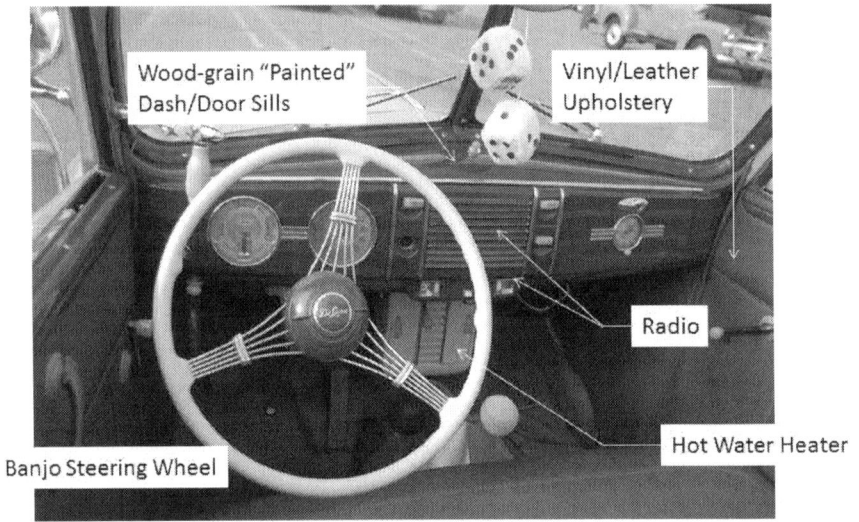

View of the interior of the restored 1939 Ford Convertible Coupe Deluxe
Photo by Author

Author displaying restored 1939 Ford Convertible Coupe at a cruise-in.
Photo by Author

There is no body panel that is flat on the old car. My wife, Marilyn, is standing next to the Ford.

Photo by Author

Marilyn gave me a 50<sup>th</sup> birthday party. Of course, the 1939 Ford was also 50 years old. The photo, below, was taken of the 50<sup>th</sup> birthday party cake.

I think the front wheel alignment is off. Photo by Author

My extended family is posing in the 1939 Ford Convertible Coupe Deluxe.
Photo by Author

Marilyn and I spent our first winter in retirement, December 2001 through March 2002, in a rented condo in Delray Beach, Florida. I had always wanted a 1950s convertible and was surfing the internet, thoroughly bored, looking at antique cars for sale on eBay. Suddenly, there appeared a listing and photographs for a 1956 Oldsmobile Starfire. This was the identification given to the Oldsmobile 98 Convertible. I told Marilyn, "Wow, I could be interested in that." She told me to go for it. She didn't have to tell me twice.

I Purchased the Car

I found an email address in the eBay listing, and contacted the owner. He and the car were located less than four miles from where I was sitting. I was in Delray Beach, Florida and the car was in Boca Raton. I drove over to look at the car, while Marilyn sat in our Honda.

It was immediately evident that there was a fuel delivery problem, as the engine needed to be cranked excessively before it fired. Then, the engine didn't take the fuel readily under acceleration. Also, the automatic transmission shifted very hard going into 3$^{rd}$ gear.

As the body, upholstery, and paint were in excellent condition, I decided to bid on the car. This was my first experience with eBay, so I was uncertain of the procedure. I waited until the last five minutes, and put my bid in. I didn't appreciate that I needed to submit a credit card number to validate my bid, because of the high value, and that ate up precious minutes. My bid broke through the reserve, I was high bidder, and I bought the car. The purchase price was $30,000. I was determined not to pay for the car out of family funds. I went back to work at GE, as a retiree callback, in my former specialty, during the summer, to earn the money to pay for the car. It took one whole summer and half the next to finish paying for the Oldsmobile.

Statistics

Nickname:    Big Bertha (Marilyn and I named her.)

Engine:    324 Cubic Inch Overhead Valve V-8, 240 HP with 4 Barrel Rochester Carburetor; "Oldsmobile Rocket Engine."

Transmission:    Jetaway 4 speed Automatic

Weight:    4325 lbs.

Cost when new:    $3740 in 1956

Quantity Built:    8531

Power Assists:    Windows, Brakes, Steering, Seats, Radio Antenna, and Convertible Top

Gas Requirement:    High Test

A friend commented, "The good news is this car has all power accessories. The bad news is they are all first generation."

This is our 1956 Oldsmobile Starfire. The colors are bold red and white. Photo by Author

Differences between the 1955 and 1956 Oldsmobile
Dash Gages
The 1955 Oldsmobile was the last model equipped with dash gages; namely the oil pressure, engine coolant temperature and generator charging gages.  In 1956, Oldsmobile changed to "idiot" lights.  These red lights illuminated when the generator was discharging, engine coolant temperature was too high or engine oil pressure was too low.  Frankly, I preferred the full gage setup, but when the 1956 Starfire presented itself, I had to buy it.

Engine in the Oldsmobile Starfire (Olds 98 convertible)

| | Displacement | HP | Torque |
|---|---|---|---|
| 1955 Engine | 324 cubic in. | 202 @4000 rpm | 332 lb. feet @ 2400 rpm |
| 1956 Engine | 324 cubic in. | 240 @4400 rpm | 350 lb. feet @ 2800 rpm |

The engine developed the extra power by virtue of thinner cylinder head gaskets, resulting in a change in compression ratio from 8.5:1 to 9.25:1.  Also, the 1956 model now required premium fuel.

Interesting technical facts
The studs that secured the wheels to the car utilized left hand threads on the left side and right hand threads on the right side.  Modern mechanics would have a difficult time removing the wheels without this knowledge.  Using conventional wisdom, the mechanic would attempt to break the fastener torque by turning the left side nuts counterclockwise.  This results in tightening the nuts rather than loosening them.

There were two foot control switches on the driver's side floor.  One controlled the headlight high and low beam.  The other changed the radio station to the next preset station.  I learned about this the hard way while driving at night.  I tried unsuccessfully to change the headlight beam. It was not until I stopped the car and looked at the floor that I realized the switch I was depressing controlled the radio station.

## Making the Car Roadworthy

I contracted with Exotic Auto Transport of Orlando, Florida to transport the car to my home in Massachusetts. Exotic had a fleet of specially-designed enclosed auto transporters to move antique, classic and exotic cars. The cost was approximately $1100. Upon returning home, I nursed the car to a friend and retired auto mechanic, to straighten out the problems, as follows:

Although the carburetor had been professionally rebuilt, it had a defective (but new) accelerator pump umbrella seal. When the throttle was pumped to deliver a squirt of fuel, the "umbrella" collapsed rather than pushing the fuel, and the fuel simply cycled around the seal.

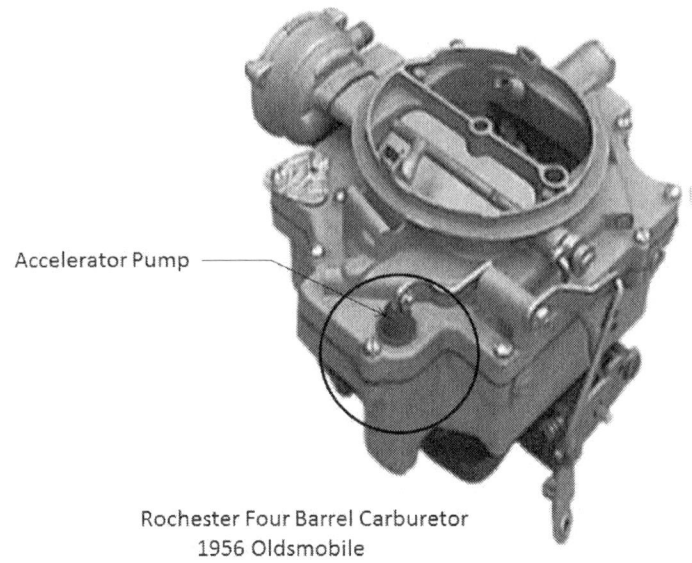

Accelerator Pump

Rochester Four Barrel Carburetor
1956 Oldsmobile

Rochester Quadrajet Carburetor[73]

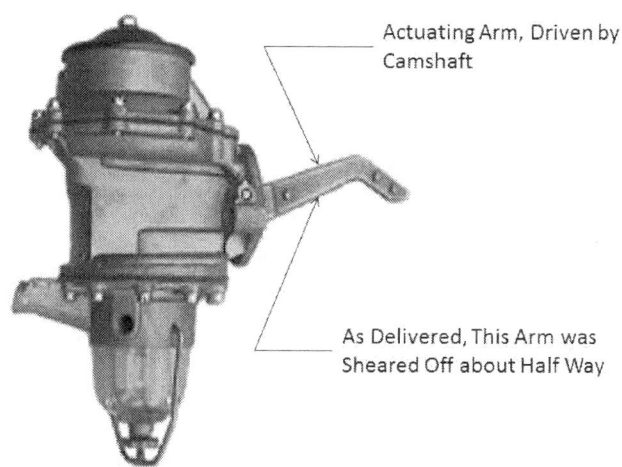

Actuating Arm, Driven by Camshaft

As Delivered, This Arm was Sheared Off about Half Way

Mechanical Fuel Pump
1956 Oldsmobile

1956 Oldsmobile mechanical fuel pump[74]

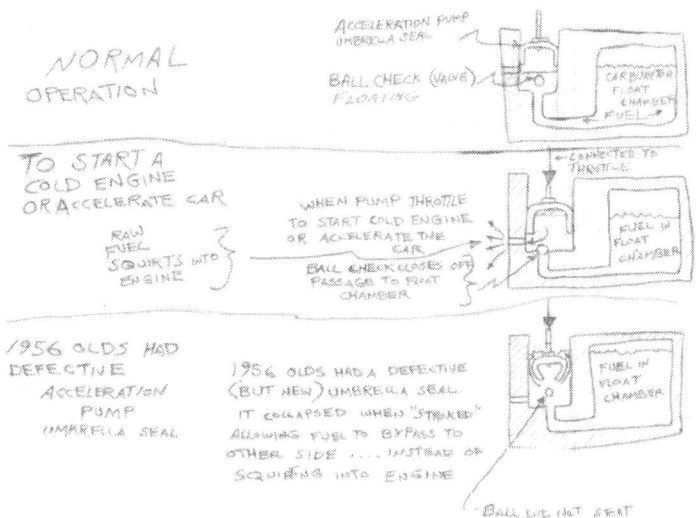

The rebuilt carburetor had a defective (but new) accelerator pump umbrella seal. When the throttle was pumped to deliver a squirt of fuel, the "umbrella" collapsed rather than pushing the fuel, and the fuel simply cycled around the seal. Sketch by Author

The vacuum advance diaphragm was compromised (failed).

74

The mechanical fuel pump was inoperative because the lever was too short. It looked like it was sheared off and it definitely was not being activated by the camshaft. I learned this when I shut off the electric fuel pump, and the engine would not run, due to fuel starvation. I discovered the "short lever" condition when I purchased a rebuilt mechanical fuel pump, and removed the old one. The car also had an electric fuel pump, as an accessory, and it was the primary and only operating pump. I pray that the missing length of pump lever is not on the bottom of the oil pan.

The transmission was another story. I contracted with Lee Miles Transmission of Dedham, Massachusetts to tear it down and rebuild it. Steve at Lee Miles was the technical editor for old Hydra-Matic Drive transmissions for the Pontiac Antique Car Club of America, so I trusted his expertise. My transmission was called "Jetaway." It relied on a second torque converter to fill or drain the transmission fluid to shift from 1$^{st}$ to 2$^{nd}$ and from 3$^{rd}$ to 4$^{th}$. Second to third relied on the conventional band, and that was the shift that was hard. It took the whole summer to straighten the Jetaway out, including locating another transmission case, but when it was done, it was right. The cost was just under $2000.

The Addition of "Super" to the Transmission
The Oldsmobile Super 88 and 98 (including the Starfire, which was the Oldsmobile 98 convertible) had what appeared to be an extra gear in the automatic transmission. On the transmission selector, the option "S" was added to P, N, Dr, Lo and R. The Oldsmobile marketing department advertised this as an additional gear called "Super." When the driver wanted to strongly accelerate, the gear shift lever was positioned to "S" and the car shifted into "Super" allowing the car to strongly accelerate. It was all marketing hype. Positioning the gearshift to "S" simply dropped the transmission gear to third gear and prevented it from shifting back to fourth, thereby allowing the engine to accelerate the car faster than in the higher gear. There was no extra "Super" gear! Bless the marketing department.

1956 Oldsmobile Jetaway Brochure[75]

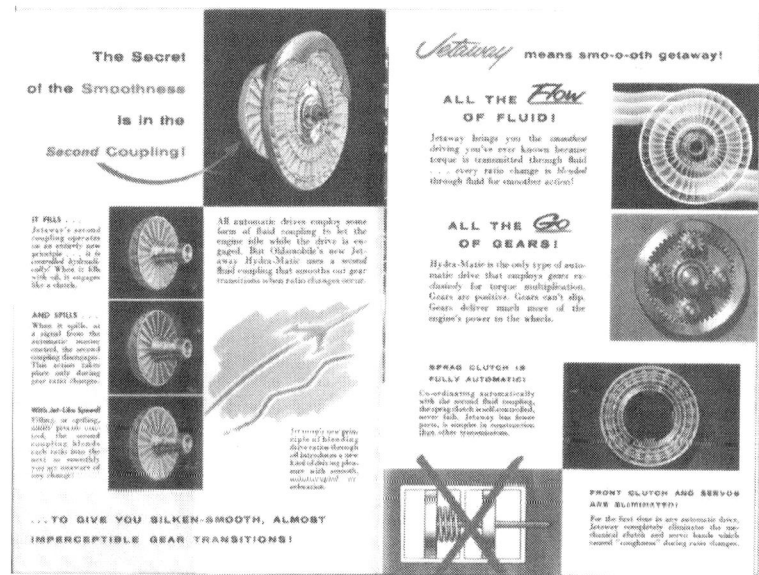

1956 Oldsmobile Jetaway Transmission Brochure[76]

75

76

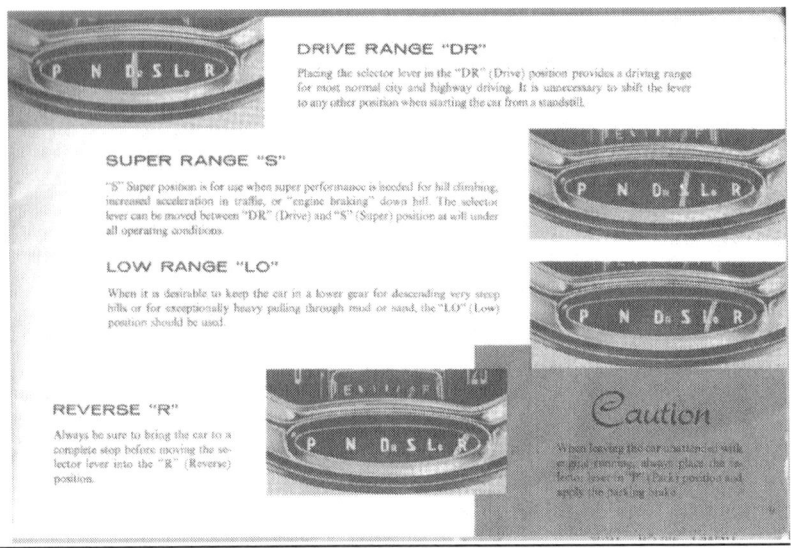

Extract from 1956 Oldsmobile Owner's Manual[77]

## The Restoration Shop

The car had been restored by a large auto restoration company, I believe "on speculation." It had been disassembled, had some metal restoration work done, and was painted. It then sat around in the shop disassembled for about two years. They must have rushed the reassembly, because they took too many shortcuts. When the shop got sick of looking at the disassembled car in their shop, someone of authority must have said, "Get that!&** thing out of here," and assigned the person with the lowest hourly pay rate to put it together. I purchased the car from an individual (who purchased the car from the restoration shop), who had business contacts with a major auto franchise, and I know he tried to have a local dealer straighten out the problems with the car. However, modern mechanics are not familiar with old cars, and the repairs didn't work out. It took many trips to my friend, the retired mechanic, to correct these errors.

In 1956, Artwork was used in promotional literature for the new cars. Later, photographs were used.

Oldsmobile promotional literature[78]

## New Convertible Top

The convertible top header didn't fit properly at the right front interface with the windshield. Whoever restored the convertible top cut the material too short, and the header, which could be adjusted, could not be moved to fit properly. Occasionally I was caught in the rain. Unfortunately, the water leaked into the car instead of shedding off. Also, there was a leakage path in the body near the trunk. The first time I experienced this was upon returning from Nova Scotia. We disembarked at Portland, Maine and stayed overnight in a motel, as we didn't want to drive the old car at night.

The next day, as we left, it started raining, and the further along we got, the harder it rained. By the time we arrived home, the carpeting was soaked. When the trunk lid was opened, water had soaked the trunk carpet, and the wheel-well that the spare tire sat in had several inches of water.

---

78

I bit the bullet and scheduled the car into a highly recommended shop, to have the top replaced. The cost estimate was $1000. A week later, I received a cell phone call, on a Sunday, from the owner's sister, who worked in the office. The workers had varnished the floor and had left the rags in a can open to the atmosphere for the weekend, when they locked up. There had been a spontaneous combustion fire in the shop over the weekend, and there was soot and smoke damage to all the cars.

It took a year, but when the insurance company straightened out the dollars, and the shop stripped and rebuilt the car, it was right as it could be. The car had originally been restored with red vinyl upholstery. The convertible shop owner felt so bad that he reinstalled the upholstery with red leather, the way the factory had originally built the car. The insurance covered all new carpeting, door panels, padded dash, trunk carpet, and so forth. The settlement was $9200. I sat down with the shop owner and we compared notes as to what he had into the car vs. the insurance check. He discounted his investment to agree with the insurance. The shop did an outstanding job.

Seat Cover Shop photo of my car as it was driven out of his shop after the soot and smoke damage.[79]

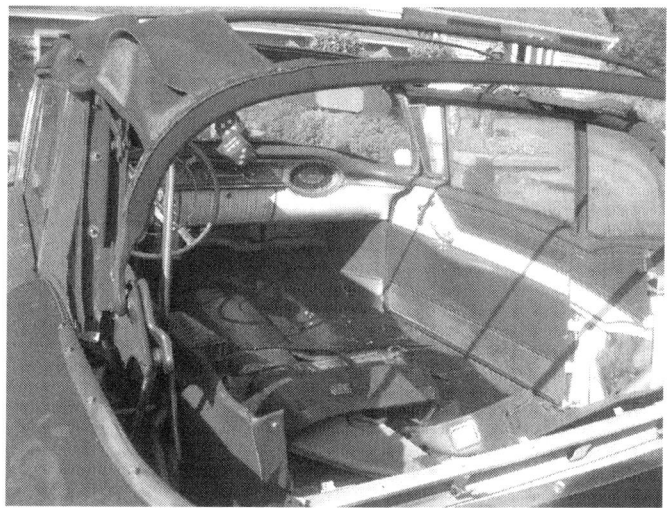

Big Bertha after the Smokey Fire[80]

## Radial Tires Were Dry Rotted

I prepared the car for an end-of-the-year car show in New Hampshire. While cleaning the wide whitewalls, I noticed some fine cracks oriented radially around one tire. Close inspection revealed that all four tires had the cracks. I called the tire manufacturer, and explained that I was not the original owner, but that the tires had probably less than 1000 miles on them.

80

The service department stepped right up and sent me four new radial whitewalls at no charge. My cost was to replace the tires on their rims, and to ship the defective tires back to the factory. I was treated very fairly by the tire manufacturer.

A Restored Car is not Always Completely Restored
One thing I learned about buying a restored car. It is never really 100% restored unless you do the restoration yourself. The next five years were spent pecking away at all the errors of omission and screw-ups that the restoration shop had made. I replaced the windshield wiper motor, convertible top electro-hydraulic pump and actuators, power seat motor, and so forth. A restoration shop usually replaced only the items that it felt needed to be replaced. The rest of the original parts were just waiting to fail.

A perfect example of this was the rubber hose(s) on the chassis. There were many of these parts in hard-to-see places that I observed needed replacement. All the parts were inexpensive, readily available and would have been easily replaced when the body was off the chassis. However, the shop apparently elected to retain these original parts, and now, 50 years later, the rubber was deteriorated and ready to fail. It was very difficult to replace some of these parts, and I needed the help of my friend, a retired mechanic, who knew the practical shortcuts.

Chronic Problem with Brakes
I had complained about the power brakes for several years. One year, Marilyn and I took the car on a tour to Nova Scotia with the NSOCC. We drove to South Portland, Maine, where the car was loaded onto the overnight ferry, "The Scotia Prince," for the boat ride to Yarmouth, Nova Scotia.

We enjoyed touring with the car, until, several days later, I was following a 1960 Chevrolet convertible down a long hill terminating at a stop light, in Halifax, Nova Scotia. After riding the brakes for a while, to maintain my distance, I attempted to actually stop the car before hitting the Chevy at the light. It was then that I experienced complete brake fade. The car had a nice hard brake pedal but had no braking action. I stopped just barely before hitting the Chevy. After the brakes cooled down, they behaved normally.

When I returned home, back I went to my friend, the mechanic. When the rear wheels were pulled, he noted that the rear brake shoes were soaked with differential fluid. Both rear wheel seals were failed, and I was braking using only the front brakes. I had been driving the car this way ever since purchase, several years ago! Obviously, when the car was "restored" the shop elected to skip replacing the rear wheel seals.

My 1956 Oldsmobile Starfire lined up in South Portland, Maine, prior to boarding the ferry to Nova Scotia. Photo by Author

Same pose as above

My 1956 Oldsmobile Starfire was on tour in Nova Scotia.  Photo by Author

At the Car show in Nova Scotia, a trophy was awarded to my 1956 Oldsmobile for the best pre-60s car.  Photo by Author

## Power Brakes

I still was not happy with the braking action, and several seasons later, the pedal was now almost to the floor. I was nervous getting under this heavy car, either on jack stands or on homemade ramps, so I decided to seek professional help. The problem was with the right-rear steel brake line. It obviously was new, but was more or less a straight shot, and was just long enough to make the connection, but not long enough to actually seal with the mating part. It had been weeping for years, until too much air got in the system. Replacement of the line and a good bleeding of the brake system gave me the pedal hardness I never had since I bought the car. Finally, the power brakes worked the way I remembered from the 1950s.

## More on 10% Ethanol in Gasoline

Along came 10% ethanol in the gas. Modern cars had no problem with the ethanol, as they used rubber parts in their fuel systems that were compatible with the fuel. Also, the computer controlled fuel injection handled the ethanol better than older cars with carburetors. But for the old cars, the fuel stayed fresh for as little as 30 days before the alcohol started to come out of solution and attract water. Old cars that were not used regularly had problems with rust and debris in the fuel tank.

Also, ethanol deteriorated the rubber parts that were in the old car's fuel system. Suddenly, most old cars were having major problems with the gas. Additives such as Stabil are available that help, but old cars continue to have problems.

My first experience with the quality of the gas came one year when I took the car out of winter storage. After charging the battery, I started the engine. It ran fine for a couple of minutes, but then ran erratically. I checked everything in the ignition system, and everything checked out. As I was out of ideas, I decided to pump the gas tank nearly empty, using my electric fuel pump and three gas cans I purchased for this purpose. With a nearly empty gas tank, I drove the car to a nearby gas station and filled the tank with fresh high-test gas. As soon as I drove the car away, the engine smoothed out and ran as originally advertised.

## Engine Cleanout Procedure

A couple of years ago, once again I was complaining about the poorly running engine. Back to my retired mechanic, I went. He put the engine on his dynamometer, and told me that I had several valves that were not working properly. I envisioned dollar bills floating out of my wallet. He told me of an old-timer's trick. He had me purchase a quart of two-cycle engine oil and mix it with five gallons of gas. Then he had me put this combination in the gas tank and fill the rest of the tank with gas. I was to take the car on a highway trip to burn up the mixture in the gas tank. Since I was going to a car event in New Hampshire that weekend, I followed his recommendation. Immediately, the engine didn't run correctly on the gas mixture. The engine ran even worse when I got on the back roads in New Hampshire, and encountered stops at traffic lights.

I nursed the car home and continued to burn most of the gas in the tank. I thought that when I added fresh gas to the nearly empty gas tank that the engine would suddenly run great. It didn't happen. The engine continued to run poorly. My mechanic was consulted by telephone. He told me to turn the two carburetor mixture screws all the way in until they bottomed, while counting the number of turns. Then, remove the screws altogether, and use my compressor and air gun to blow out any debris in the carburetor through the two holes where the mixture screws were. Then put the screws back to the same number of turns that I had counted originally. As soon as I started the engine, the improvement in engine performance was obvious. I have had to perform this procedure several times, about once per year, to blow out the debris from the ethanol gas in the carburetor.

## Nightmare Tour to a Fifties Diner in New Hampshire

The NSOCC had a trip to a 1950s diner in Rochester, New Hampshire. It was a beautiful sunny Sunday, and I did not check the weather forecast. This was a big mistake. The group met at a rest stop on Interstate 95 North near the New Hampshire border. The cars departed convoy style, and the further we drove into New Hampshire the darker the sky appeared in the west. Soon, there was lightning in the distance.

Then the storm was upon us with wind gusts and heavy rain. There were tree limbs on the ground as we continued, but we made it to the diner.

After lunch, we were given directions back to a major highway, and set out individually to go home. We didn't get more than a half mile before we encountered fallen trees and a detour sign. We were detoured into a residential neighborhood and then the detour signs disappeared. We were on our own and were lost until one car from our group, a 1972 Ford, was observed going in the opposite direction. We decided that the driver of the Ford knew where he was going, and reversed course and followed him.

Then it started raining again, and it became worse. The windows were fogged up and visibility was poor. It seemed like hours, heading west down back roads, looking for any sign to a major north-south highway. Finally, we spotted a fire station and pulled into the parking lot. The station was open but unoccupied. However, there was a map on the wall, and we saw US Route 28, a major North-South road. It was just one more block.

Handsome 1956 Oldsmobile Dash. Photo by Author

The car burned most of a whole tank of gas that day, and once again the car rugs and trunk were soaked with rain. It was my fault for not checking the weather forecast. It was a valuable lesson, and I now religiously check the weather before taking out Big Bertha.

Antique Car Meet in Newburyport, Massachusetts
One Sunday, I was driving the Oldsmobile, up US Route 1 North, on my way to an antique car meet in Newburyport. It was a beautiful morning and I was stuck behind a slow driver on this winding two-lane undivided road. He was taking his time, and I couldn't see around him far enough to chance passing him. Finally, the road straightened out long enough for me to be able to pass. I pulled out and dumped the throttle to pass. I sailed past the slow driver, and, as I was about to move back into my lane, I was aware that the Oldsmobile was accelerating much too fast for my comfort. I quickly slowed down. The powerful car got away from me. Now, I am aware of the power available and am more careful while accelerating.

"I had the exact same car.."
I have displayed the Oldsmobile at many Cruise-ins while living in The Villages, Florida. At every event, I have at least one spectator regale about how he had the exact same car, at one time. Except for the fact the car was a 1954 Oldsmobile, a four door sedan and painted green and white. Other than that, it was the exact same car!

My out-of-date Massachusetts safety inspection sticker
About May 2013, the Oldsmobile was on display at the monthly Cruise-in. A spectator observed my out-of-date Massachusetts inspection sticker. He inquired if I was from Massachusetts. I replied in the affirmative.

He told me he was from Worcester. My mother's whole family was from Worcester. His father owned Tagman's Bakery at 59 Providence Street, in Worcester, from 1939 through the 1950s. He told me that the building had sat vacant for several years before his father bought it.

I replied that my grandfather owned a kosher bakery on Providence Street, but had lost the business in 1935, after which the building sat vacant for several years. After checking with several cousins, who grew up in Worcester, and comparing an old photograph of the bakery exterior with one provided of Tagman's Bakery, we both concluded that the building was one and the same. What a small world. We were brought together by my 1956 Oldsmobile.

### Car replacement cost appraisal
Before I moved to The Villages, in 2011, I had the Oldsmobile professionally appraised. I raised the insured value to agree with the professional appraisal of $75,000. Ten years ago I purchased the car on eBay for $30,000. That was not a bad investment, considering the fun that I had with the car over the ten years of ownership.

### The Moral or Conclusion of the Story
What is the moral or conclusion of the story? There is no moral and definitely no conclusion. I am in a hobby that is more obsession than hobby. We car nuts buy what we remember, and we do what we can to keep them running, and enjoy them as much as possible. Oh yes, this car was manufactured the year that I graduated high school. I drove the car to my 50th high school reunion, Class of 1956! The car was the hit of the reunion.

My 1956 Oldsmobile Starfire with top down
Photo by Author

Photo by Author

t. P. Dronfield
27 Hampshire Rd.
Peabody, MA 01960
USA

I have some informations for your
Danish build Ford.
That nameplate you mention is
riveted on the floor on the left side.
I have a 1935 model but I am sure
the nameplate is placed alike on your
1939. See photo.
But there are other differences against
an American built car. You are not supposed to have the car number plate nor the
patent plate, but the rivet holes (sic) are
there. In the upper left corner of the
firewall is a little oval nameplate
placed with two rivets. See photo.
All cars in Scandinavia and perhaps
more european countries was fitted with
those turn signals. All Ford cars before
WW II was fitted with "WEIKRA" signals.
I cannot give you any sure information
of the outch. I think there has been

a lot of different switches during the years. Maybe you have an extra hole in your dashboard where a little two way switch has been mounted. After WW II? There was another type of switch mounted on the steering column just under the steering wheel with automatic return.

How come an Danish assembled Ford has found its way to America? Danish cars are often badly rusted because of all under-coating, mine was very bad too but I have done most of the sheet metal job now.

I am interested having the nameplate if you have spares.

*Roland Swalas*

ROLAND SWALAS
VILLAVAGEN 27
53155 LIDKOPING
SWEDEN

This letter was from Roland Swalas of Sweden. He clarified the unusual nameplate that mounted on the engine firewall, as well as the location of the export data plate. The envelope was date stamped March 27, 1986.

Roland's Danish 1935 Ford Roadster with trafficators

Roland has passed away, but his sister and brother-in-law have given permission to publish his letter and photo of his 1935 Danish Ford Roadster.

Magazine of the Early Ford Club of America

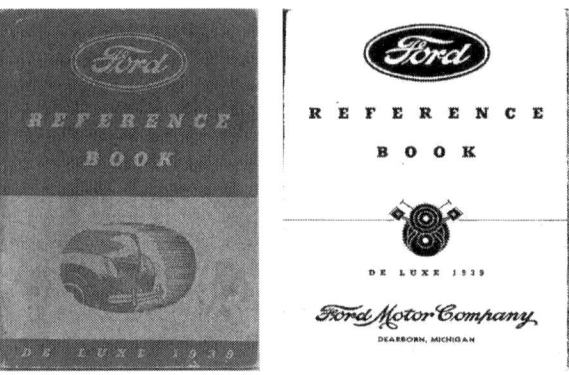

Original Owners Manual 1939 Ford DeLuxe

The Owner's Manual for the 1939 Ford Standard is being reproduced, but this Owner's Manual for the Deluxe must be located in original condition.

# FORD V-8 DELUXE

## Warranty

The Ford Motor Company warrants all such parts of new Ford automobiles, trucks and chassis, except tires, (see warranty below covering tires manufactured by Ford Motor Company) for a period of ninety (90) days from the date of original delivery to the purchaser of each new Ford vehicle or before such vehicle has been driven 4,000 miles, whichever event shall first occur, as shall, under normal use and service, appear to it to have been defective in workmanship or material. This warranty shall be limited to shipment, to the purchaser without charge, except for transportation, of the part or parts intended to replace those acknowledged by the Ford Motor Company to be defective. The Ford Motor Company cannot, however, and does not accept any responsibility in connection with any of its automobiles, trucks or chassis when they have been altered outside of its own factories or branch plants. If the purchaser shall use or allow to be used in the automobile, truck or chassis, parts not made or supplied by the Ford Motor Company, then this warranty shall become void. The Ford Motor Company does not undertake responsibility to any purchaser of its products for any undertaking, representation or warranty made by dealers selling its products, beyond those herein expressed.

The Ford Motor Company reserves the right to make changes in design and changes or improvements upon its product without imposing any obligation upon itself to install the same upon its products theretofore manufactured.

## Tire Warrranty

Every tire manufactured by the Ford Motor Company and bearing its name and serial number is warranted by it to be free from defects in workmanship and material, without limit as to time or mileage, and to give satisfactory service under normal operating conditions. If Ford Motor Company's examination shows that any tire has failed under the terms of this warranty, it will at its option either repair the tire or make an allowance on the purchase of a new tire.

Extract from the 1939 Ford Owner's Manual

Hængende i Transportbaand glider Karosserierne gennem Malerværkstederne, medens de gennemgaar de mange forskellige Behandlinger.

Sadelmageren gennemskærer 50 Lag Betrækstof paa een Gang.

Et Hjørne af Sadelmagerværkstederne.

Fords assembled in the Copenhagen factory
Captions are in Danish

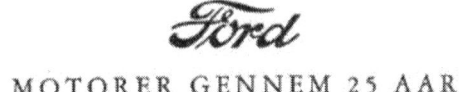

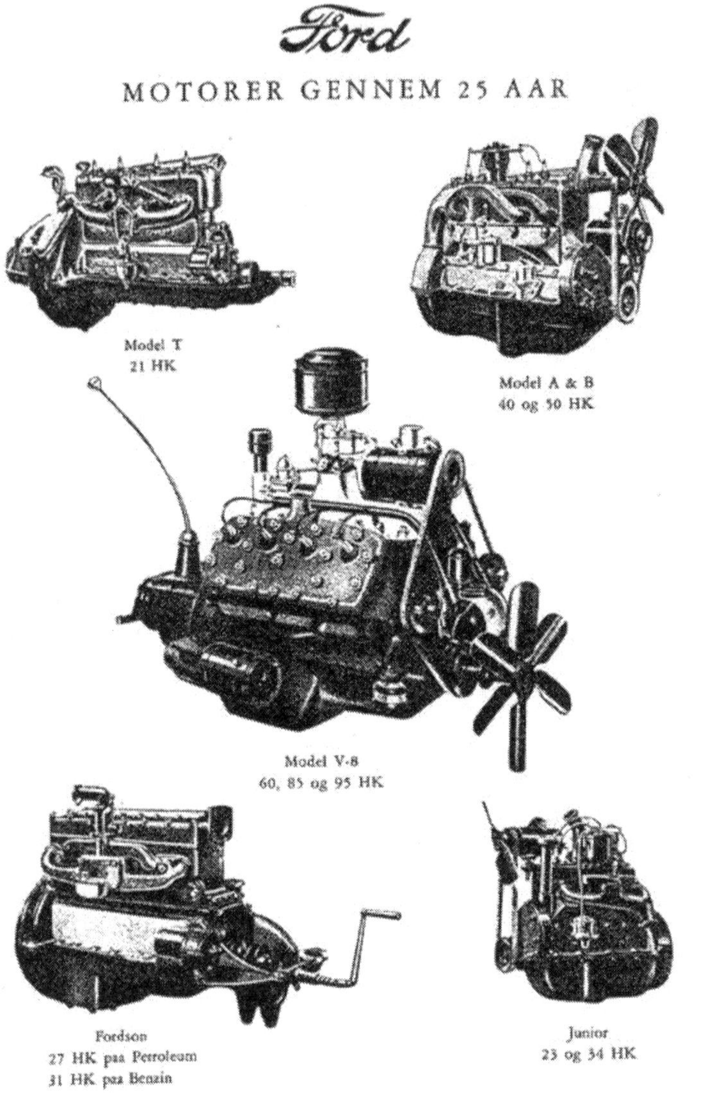
Ford
MOTORER GENNEM 25 AAR
Model T
21 HK
Model A & B
40 og 50 HK
Model V-8
60, 85 og 95 HK
Fordson
27 HK paa Petroleum
31 HK paa Benzin
Junior
23 og 34 HK

Engines installed in Danish Fords. The Flathead engine in the middle went with my car. Captions are in Danish

# Notes

1     en.wikipedia.org/wiki/Chrysler_New_Yorker
2     en.wikipedia.org/wiki/1941_Ford
3     en.wikipedia.org/wiki/1949_Ford
4     en.wikipedia.org/wiki/1955_Ford
5     en.wikipedia.org/wiki/Chevrolet_Deluxe
6     en.wikipedia.org/wiki/Chevrolet_Bel_Air
7     en.wikipedia.org/wiki/Amphicar
      en.wikipedia.org/wiki/king_Midget
8     en.wikipedia.org/wiki/Nash_Statesman
9     http://en.wikipedia.org/wiki/Lincoln_Industrial_Corporation
10   en.wikipedia.org/wiki/Chevrolet_Corvette_(C1)
      en.wikipedia.org/wiki/Ford_Thunderbird
      en.wikipedia.org/wiki/Studebaker_Avanti
      en.wikipedia.org/wiki/Kaiser_Darrin
11   en.wikipedia.org/wiki/1941_Ford1942
12   en.wikipedia.org/wiki/1949_Ford
13   en.wikipedia.org/wiki/Ford_Model_A_(1927-1931)
      en.wikipedia.org/wiki/1937_Ford
      en.wikipedia.org/wiki/1949_Ford
      en.wikipedia.org/wiki/1960_Ford
14   en.wikipedia.org/wiki/1949_Ford
15   en.wikipedia.org/wiki/Pontiac_Straight-8_engine
16   flicker.com
17   flicker.com
18   en.wikipedia.org/wiki/Radial_tire
19   Ford Reference Book, De Luxe 1939, Figure 18, Pg. 32/33
20   en.wikipedia.org/wiki/Hill-holder
21   http://www.popularmechanics.com/cars/news/auto-blog/carchaeology-1952-oldsmobile-and-the-first-headlight-dimmer-16301766
22   en.wikipedia.org/wiki/Snow_chains
23   en.wikipedia.org/wiki/Air_filter
24   www.cficonnect.com
25   en.wikipedia.org/wiki/Pontiac_Streamliner
26   1940 LaSalle Series 50 flickr.com
27   Old Cars Weekly, dated December 5, 1985 Dated November 1950
28   Photo by Author at Hershey AACA National Meet
29   1940 Ford DeLuxe Wikimedia Commons
30   Ford Chassis Parts and Accessories Catalogue
      Passenger Cars 1928 thru 1948 – Trucks 1928 thru 1947
      Dated November 1950, Pg. 349
31   Ford Reference Book, De Luxe 1939, Figure 18, Pg. 59
32   Ford Reference Book, De Luxe 1939, Figure 6, Pg. 17
33   Ford Reference Book, De Luxe 1939
34   Ford Reference Book, De Luxe 1939, Figure 11, Pg. 23
35   www.bobdrake.com

| 36 | Ford Reference Book, De Luxe 1939, Figure 10, Pg. 22 |
| 37 | Ford Reference Book, De Luxe 1939, Figure 16, Pg. 29 |
| 38 | Ford Reference Book, De Luxe 1939, Figure 24, Pg. 45 |
| 39 | Ford Chassis Parts and Accessories Catalogue |
| | Passenger Cars 1928 thru 1948 – Trucks 1928 thru 1947 |
| | Dated November 1950, Pg 758 |
| 40 | Ford Chassis Parts and Accessories Catalogue |
| | Passenger Cars 1928 thru 1948 – Trucks 1928 thru 1947 |
| | Dated November 1950 |
| 41 | en.wikipedia.org/wiki/1941_Ford |
| 42 | Ford, 1939 and 1940 Engine & Chassis Repair Manual, Polyprints, Books about Ford |
| 43 | Ford Chassis Parts and Accessories Catalogue |
| | Passenger Cars 1928 thru 1948 – Trucks 1928 thru 1947 |
| | Dated November 1950 |
| 44 | Photo by Precision Coachworks, Billerica, Ma. |
| 45 | The V-8 Album, Early Ford V-8 Club of America, Pg. 143 |
| 46 | Photo by Precision Coachworks, Billerica, Ma. |
| 47 | bradleyfloorpans.com/39-40.0.html |
| 48 | Photo by Precision Coachworks, Billerica, Ma. |
| 49 | Photo by Precision Coachworks, Billerica, Ma. |
| 50 | Photo by Precision Coachworks, Billerica, Ma |
| 51 | Photo by Precision Coachworks, Billerica, Ma |
| 52 | Photo by Precision Coachworks, Billerica, Ma |
| 53 | Photo by Precision Coachworks, Billerica, Ma |
| 54 | Photo by Precision Coachworks, Billerica, Ma |
| 55 | Photo by Precision Coachworks, Billerica, Ma |
| 56 | Photo by Precision Coachworks, Billerica, Ma |
| 57 | Ford, 1939 and 1940 Engine & Chassis Repair Manual, Polyprints, Books about Ford, Pg. 39 |
| 58 | en.wikipedia.org/wiki/Lincoln_Continental |
| 59 | www.marvelmysteryoil.com |
| 60 | Ford Chassis Parts and Accessories Catalogue |
| | Passenger Cars 1928 thru 1948 – Trucks 1928 thru 1947 |
| | Dated November 1950, Pg. 88 |
| 61 | Ford Chassis Parts and Accessories Catalogue |
| | Passenger Cars 1928 thru 1948 – Trucks 1928 thru 1947 |
| | Dated November 1950, Pg. 114 |
| 62 | www.macsautoparts.com/ |
| 63 | dennis-carpenter.com/trk32-47coils/c/189/ |
| 64 | en.wikipedia.org/wiki/Scotia_Prince_Cruises |
| 65 | Ford Reference Book, De Luxe 1939 |
| 66 | Collection owned by Mike Dingman, at the time |
| 67 | Photo provided by Mike Dingman |
| 68 | Ford Reference Book, De Luxe 1939, Figure 22, Pg. 40 |
| 69 | www.allpar.com/old/oils.php |
| 70 | blog.hemmings.com/index.php/2012/10/18/tech-101-zinc-in-oil-and-its-effects-on-older-engines/ |

| | |
|---|---|
| 71 | batteryuniversity.com/learn/article/sulfation_and_how_to_prevent_it |
| 72 | Ford Field for October 1951 |
| 73 | www.fusick.com |
| | Fusick Catalogue#570, Pg. 38 |
| 74 | www.fusick.com |
| | Fusick Catalogue#570, Pg. 39 |
| 75 | 1956 Oldsmobile Promotional Literature |
| 76 | 1956 Oldsmobile Promotional Literature |
| 77 | 1956 Oldsmobile Promotional Literature |
| 78 | 1956 Oldsmobile Promotional Literature |
| 79 | Photo provided by Columbia Seat Cover Co., Haverhill, Ma. |
| 80 | Photo provided by Columbia Seat Cover Co., Haverhill, Ma. |

11497641R00116

Printed in Great Britain
by Amazon.co.uk, Ltd.,
Marston Gate.